Guitar Tab Edition

The Great Escape...

MCA Music Limited

Exclusive Distributors:
Music Sales Limited
8/9 Frith Street, London W1V 5TZ, England.
Music Sales Pty Limited
120 Rothschild Avenue, Rosebery, NSW 2018, Australia.

Order No. AM934780
ISBN 0-7119-5463-1
This book © Copyright 1995 by MCA Music Limited.

Original LP cover design by Stylo Rouge.
Book design by Michael Bell Design.
Music arranged by Arthur Dick.
Music processed by The Pitts.
Front cover photograph courtesy of The Image Bank.
Back cover photograph courtesy of Nels Israelson.

Printed in the United Kingdom by
Caligraving Limited, Thetford, Norfolk.

Stereotypes

THE SUBURBS THEY ARE DREAMING
THEY ARE A TWINKLE IN HER EYE
SHE'S BEEN FEELING FRISKY
SINCE HER HUSBAND SAID GOODBYE
SHE WEARS A LOW CUT T-SHIRT RUNS A LITTLE B&B
SHE MOST ACCOMMODATING WHEN SHE'S IN HER LINGERIE

WIFE SWAPPING IS THE FUTURE
YOU KNOW THAT IT WOULD SUIT YOU

YES, THEY'RE STEREOTYPES
THERE MUST BE MORE TO LIFE
ALL YOUR LIFE YOU ARE DREAMING
FROM TIME TO TIME YOU KNOW
YOU SHOULD BE GOING ON ANOTHER BENDER

THE SUBURBS THEY ARE SLEEPING
BUT HE'S DRESSING UP TONIGHT
SHE LIKES A MAN IN UNIFORM HE LOVES TO WEAR IT TIGHT
THEY ARE ON THE LOVERS SOFA THEY ARE ON THE PATIO
AND WHEN THE FUN IS OVER WATCH THEMSELVES ON VIDEO

THE NEIGHBOURS MAY BE STARING
BUT THEY ARE JUST PAST CARING

Best Days

BOW BELLS SAY GOODBYE TO THE LAST TRAIN
OVER THE RIVER THEY ALL GO AGAIN
OUT INTO LEAFY NOWHERE HOPE SOMEONE
WAITING OUT THERE FOR THEM
CABBIE HAS HIS MIND ON A FARE TO THE SUN
HE WORKS NIGHT BUT IT'S NOT MUCH FUN
PICKS UP THE LONDON YOYO'S, ALL ON THEIR OWN DOWN SOHO
PLEASE TAKE ME HOME

OTHER PEOPLE WOULDN'T WANT TO HEAR YOU
IF YOU SAID THAT THESE ARE THE BEST DAYS OF THEIR LIVES
OTHER PEOPLE WOULD TURN AROUND AND LAUGH AT YOU
IF YOU SAID THAT THESE WERE THE BEST DAYS OF OUR LIVES

TRELLICK TOWERS BEEN CALLING
I KNOW SHE'LL LEAVE ME IN THE MORNING

IN HOTEL CELLS LISTENING TO DIAL TONES
REMOTE CONTROLS AND CABLE MOANS
IN HIS DRINK HE'S BEEN TALKING
GETS DISCONNECTED SLEEPWALKING BACK HOME

Country House

(SO THE STORY BEGINS)
CITY DWELLER, SUCCESSFUL FELLA
THOUGHT TO HIMSELF
OOPS I'VE GOT ALOT OF MONEY
I'M CAUGHT IN A RAT RACE TERMINALLY
I'M A PROFESSIONAL CYNIC
BUT MY HEARTS NOT IN IT
I'M PAYING THE PRICE OF LIVING LIFE AT THE LEGAL LIMIT
CAUGHT UP IN THE CENTURIES ANXIETY
IT PREYS ON HIM, HE'S GETTING THIN

NOW HE LIVES IN A HOUSE, A VERY BIG HOUSE IN THE COUNTRY
WATCHING AFTERNOON REPEATS
AND THE FOOD HE EATS IN THE COUNTRY
HE TAKES ALL MANNER OF PILLS
AND PILES UP ANALYST BILLS IN THE COUNTRY
IT'S LIKE AN ANIMAL FARM,
LOTS OF RURAL CHARM IN THE COUNTRY

NOW HE'S GOT MORNING GLORY, LIFE'S A DIFFERENT STORY
EVERYTHING GOING JACKANORY
IN TOUCH WITH HIS OWN MORALITY
HE'S READING BALZAC, KNOCKING BACK PROZAC,
IT'S A HELPING HAND
THAT MAKES YOU FEEL WONDERFULLY BLAND
OH, IT'S THE CENTURIES REMEDY FOR THE FAINT AT HEART
A NEW START

HE LIVES IN A HOUSE, A VERY BIG HOUSE IN THE COUNTRY
HE'S GOT A FOG IN HIS CHEST
SO HE NEEDS ALOT OF REST IN THE COUNTRY
HE DOESN'T DRINK SMOKE LAUGH
HE TAKES HERBAL BATHS IN THE COUNTRY
OH, IT'S LIKE AN ANIMAL FARM
BUT YOU'LL COME TO NO HARM IN THE COUNTRY
BLOW BLOW ME OUT I AM SO SAD I DON'T KNOW WHY

Charmless Man

I MET HIM IN A CROWDED ROOM
WHERE PEOPLE GO TO DRINK AWAY THEIR GLOOM
HE SAT ME DOWN AND SO BEGAN, THE STORY OF A CHARMLESS MAN
EDUCATED THE EXPENSIVE WAY, HE KNOWS HIS CLARET FROM A BEAUJOLAIS
I THINK HE'D LIKE TO OF BEEN RONNIE KRAY
BUT THEN NATURE DIDN'T MAKE HIM THAT WAY

HE THINKS HE'S EDUCATED, AIRS THOSE FAMILY SHARES
WILL PROTECT HIM THAT WE WILL RESPECT HIM
HE MOVES IN CIRCLES OF FRIENDS
WHO JUST PRETEND THAT THEY LIKE HIM
HE DOES THE SAME TO THEM, AND WHEN YOU PUT IT ALL TOGETHER
THERE'S THE MODEL OF A CHARMLESS MAN

HE KNOWS THE SWINGERS AND THEIR CAVALRY
SAYS HE CAN GET IN ANYWHERE FOR FREE
I BEGAN TO GO A LITTLE CROSS EYED
AND FROM THIS CHARMLESS MAN I JUST HAD TO HIDE

HE TALKS AT SPEED HE GETS NOSE BLEEDS
HE DOESN'T SEE HIS DAYS
ARE TUMBLING DOWN UPON HIM
AND YET HE TRIES SO HARD TO PLEASE
HE'S JUST SO KEEN FOR YOU TO LISTEN
BUT NO ONE IS LISTENING
AND WHEN YOU PUT IT ALL TOGETHER
THERE'S THE MODEL OF A CHARMLESS MAN

The Universal

THIS IS THE NEXT CENTURY
THE UNIVERSAL IS FREE
YOU CAN FIND IT ANYWHERE
YES, THE FUTURE HAS BEEN SOLD
EVERY NIGHT WE ARE GONE
AND THE KARAOKE SONGS
WE LIKE TO SING ALONG
ALTHOUGH THE WORDS ARE WRONG

IT REALLY, REALLY, REALLY COULD HAPPEN
WHEN THE DAYS SEEM TO FALL STRAIGHT THROUGH YOU
JUST LET THEM GO

NO ONE HERE IS ALONE
SATELLITES IN EVERY HOME
THE UNIVERSAL IS HERE
HERE FOR EVERYONE
EVERY PAPER THAT YOU READ
SAYS TOMORROW IS YOUR LUCKY DAY
WELL, HERE'S YOUR LUCKY DAY

Fade Away

THEY STUMBLED INTO THEIR LIVES
IN A VAGUE WAY BECAME MAN AND WIFE
ONE GOT THE OTHER THEY DESERVED ONE ANOTHER
THEY SETTLED IN A BRAND NEW TOWN
WITH PEOPLE FROM THE SAME BACKGROUND
THEY KEPT THEMSELVES BUSY
LONGS HOURS LEFT THEM DIZZY
NOW WHEN HE'S IN SHE'S OUT

ALL YOU EVER DO IS FADE AWAY
THEY ARE NOT MAKING PLANS
BECAUSE NOW THEY UNDERSTAND
ALL YOU EVER DO IS FADE AWAY

HE NOTICED HE HAD VISIBLE LINES
SHE WORRIED ABOUT HER BEHIND
THEIR BIRTH HAD BEEN THE DEATH OF THEM
IT DIDN'T REALLY BOTHER THEM
NOW WHEN SHE'S IN, HE'S OUT

TOPMAN

THIS IS A PUBLIC WARNING
BE CAREFUL WHEN YOU ARE OUT
WE ARE HAVING FREAKY WEATHER
THERE'S ALOT OF IT ABOUT
THE TERRACES ARE SWINGING
HE'S A MONKEY ON THE ROOF
YOU'VE SEEN HIM ON THE TELLY
SO LET ME INTRODUCE YOUR HOST TONIGHT

T.O.P.M.A.N.
HE'S NAUGHTY BY NATURE
ON DOUBLES AND CHASERS
HE'S A LITTLE BOY RACER
SHOOTING GUNS ON THE HIGH STREET OF LOVE

IN A CROWD IT'S HARD TO SPOT HIM, BUT ANONYMITY CAN COST
HE'S NEVER CHEAP N' CHEERFUL, HE'S HUGO AND HE'S BOSS
HE'S RIDING THROUGH THE DESERT ON A CAMEL LIGHT
AND ON A MAGIC CARPET, HE'LL FLY AWAY TONIGHT
OPEN SESAME

T.O.P.M.A.N.
SEES HER IN DOUBLE
THEN PUKES ON THE PAVEMENT
LIKES HER ALL CLEAN AND SHAVEN
SHOOTING GUNS ON THE HIGH STREET OF LOVE

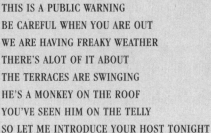

Mr. Robinson's Quango

MR. ROBINSON AND HIS QUANGO
DIRTY DEALER, EXPENSIVE CAR
RUNS THE BUSES AND THE EVENING STAR
HE GOT A HAIR PIECE AND HE GOT HERPES
HIS PRIVATE LIFE IS VERY DISCREET
A NICER MAN YOU'LL NEVER GOING TO MEET

A SELF PROFESSED SAVIOUR OF THE DIM RIGHT WING
HE'S GOT RESPITORY PROBLEMS AND A MASONS RING

MR. ROBINSON AND HIS QUANGO
DRINKS WITH THE GENERAL AND THE COUNTY WIVES
YES THE FAMILY BUSINESS IS DOING ALL RIGHT
THEY ARE DOING TANGO'S DOWN IN THE QUANGO'S
HE MAKES THEM TICK AND HE MAKES THEM TOCK
AND IF HE DOESN'T LIKE YOU HE'LL PUT YOU IN THE DOCK

HE JUST SITS IN HIS LEATHER CHAIR AND TWIDDLES HIS THUMBS
GETS HIS SECRETARY IN AND PINCHES HER BUM

HE RAN INTO THE TOILET IN THE TOWN HALL
GOT A BIRO OUT AND WROTE ON THE WALL
I'M WEARING FRENCH KNICKERS ON UNDER MY SUIT
I'VE GOT STOCKING AND SUSPENDERS ON
I'M FEELING RATHER LOOSE

OH I'M A NAUGHTY BOY
OH I'M A NAUGHTY, NAUGHTY BOY

He Thought Of Cars

MOSCOW'S STILL RED
THE YOUNG MAN'S DEAD
GONE TO HEAVEN INSTEAD
THE EVENING NEWS SAYS HE WAS CONFUSED
THE MOTORWAYS WILL ALL MERGE SOON
THEY'VE COME TO SAVE US
THE SPACE INVADERS ARE HERE

HE THOUGHT OF CARS
AND WHERE, WHERE TO DRIVE THEM
AND WHO TO DRIVE THEM WITH
AND THERE, THERE WAS NO ONE, NO ONE

THERE'S A PANIC AT LONDON HEATHROW
EVERYBODY WANTS TO GO UP INTO THE BLUE
BUT THERE'S A TEN YEAR QUEUE
COLUMBIA IS IN TOP GEAR
IT SHOULDN'T SNOW AT THIS TIME OF YEAR
NOW AMERICAS SHOT GONE
AND DONE THE LOT

HE THOUGHT OF PLANES AND WHERE
WHERE TO FLY TO
AND WHO TO FLY THERE WITH
AND THERE, THERE WAS NO ONE, NO ONE

It Could Be You

CHURCHILL GOT HIS LUCKY NUMBER
BUT TOMORROW THERE'S ANOTHER
COULD BE ME COULD BE YOU
NO SILVER SPOON
STICKY TEETH THEY ROT TOO SOON
YOU'VE GOT TO HAVE THE BEST TUNES
OR THAT'S IT YOU'VE BLOWN IT

ALL WE WANT IS TO BE HAPPY
IN OUR HOMES LIKE HAPPY FAMILIES
BE THE MAN ON THE BEACH WITH
THE WORLD AT HIS FEET
YES, IT COULD BE YOU

THE LIKELY LADS
ARE PICKING UP THE UGLIES
YESTERDAY THEY WERE JUST PUPPIES
BEERY SLURS NOW LIFE'S A BLUR
TELLY ADDICTS
YOU SHOULD SEE THEM AT IT
GETTING IN A PANIC
WILL WE BE THERE
TRAFALGAR SQUARE?

SO DON'T WORRY
IF IT'S NOT YOUR LUCKY NUMBER
BECAUSE TOMORROW THERE IS ANOTHER
COULD BE YOU, COULD BE ME

Ernold Same

ERNOLD SAME AWOKE FROM THE SAME DREAM
IN THE SAME BED AT THE SAME TIME
LOOKED IN THE SAME MIRROR
MADE THE SAME FROWN
AND FELT THE SAME WAY AS HE DID EVERY DAY,
THEN ERNOLD SAME CAUGHT THE SAME TRAIN
AT THE SAME STATION, SAT IN THE SAME SEAT
WITH THE SAME NASTY STAIN
NEXT TO SAME OLD WHAT'S HIS NAME
ON HIS WAY TO THE SAME PLACE TO DO THE SAME THING
AGAIN AND AGAIN ... POOR OLD ERNOLD SAME.
OH ERNOLD SAME,
HIS WORLDS STAYS THE SAME,
TODAY WILL ALWAYS BE TOMORROW,
POOR OLD ERNOLD SAME,
HE 'S GETTING THAT FELLING ONCE AGAIN,
NOTHING WILL CHANGE TOMORROW.

Globe Alone

WHO MADDEST ONE ON THE M1
WHO HASN'T STOPPED SUCKING HIS THUMB
WHO VERY STRAIGHT AND NEVER GRINS
WHO CARES WHAT CAR HE'S DRIVING IN

HE IS BECAUSE HE SAW IT ON A COMMERCIAL BREAK
AND IF HE DOESN'T GET WHAT
HE WANTS THEN HE'LL GET A HEADACHE
BECAUSE HE WANTS IT, NEEDS IT, ALMOST LOVES IT
HE'S HERE ON HIS OWN, ON GLOBE ALONE

WHO JOINED HEALTH CLUB TO GLISTEN
INTO HI FI PRECISION
WHO'S MOBILE PHONE GIVES HIM THE BONE
WHO VERY KEEN ON SHARON STONE

WHO ONLY EATS AT THE NEW BRASSERIE
WHO ONLY EVERY GETS MERRY
WHO WOULDN'T BE SEEN AT BED TIME
WITHOUT PUTTING CALVIN KLEINS ON

Dan Abnormal (The Meanie Leanie)

MEANIE LEANIE COME ON DOWN
COME AND ENTERTAIN THE TOWN
IT'S FRIDAY NIGHT AND WE'RE ALL BORED
TIMES BEEN CALLED THERE IS NO MORE
TIMES BEEN CALLED IT'S SUCH A BORE

DAN ABNORMAL NOT NORMAL AT ALL
IT'S NOT HIS FAULT WE MADE HIM THIS WAY
HE'LL IMITATE YOU TRY TO APE YOU
BUT IT'S NOT HIS FAULT DAN WATCHES TV

THE MEANIE LEANIE STAYS UP LATE
MOPES AROUND GETS IN A STATE
HE'S THE KILLER IN YOUR ARCADE
KILLING GANGSTAS READY MADE
CAUSE THAT IS WHERE THE FUTURES MADE

TELE PORT ME

DAN WENT TO HIS LOCAL BURGER BAR
I WANT McNORMAL AND CHIPS
OR I'LL BLOW YOU TO BITS
GIVE US IT

IT'S THE MISERIES AT HALF PAST THREE
WATCHING VIDEO NASTIES
HE HAS DIRTY DREAMS WHILE HE'S ASLEEP
DAN'S JUST LIKE YOU YOU SEE
HE'S THE MEANIE LEANIE

Entertain Me

THE WEEKEND IS BACK
BUT SO IS HE
HEAD TO THE FLOODLIGHTS
SEE THE FRATERNITY
THEY ARE WAITING
I HEAR THEM UP IN THE NORTH
AND DOWN IN THE SOUTH
ALL THAT IS SPEWING
SPEWING OUT OF HIS MOUTH

ENTERTAIN ME
AT HIS AND HERS DATING
BORED MINDS AGREE
REQUIREMENTS TO BE STATED
REPLIES AWAITED
SHE WANTS A LOOSE FIT
HE WANTS INSTANT WHIP
HE GUESSTIMATES HER ARRIVAL
WILL SHE WANT IT REALLY BADLY

ENTERTAIN ME

A CAR, A HOUSE BOTH IN STREET
THE BOREDOM OF THE SOBER WEEK
THE WEEKEND IS HERE, HIP HIP HOORAY
TO MAKE THE BLUES JUST GO AWAY

ENTERTAIN ME

Yuko and Hiro

THIS IS MY WORK PLACE
AND THESE ARE THE PEOPLE I WORK WITH
YUKO AND HIRO
WE WORK TOGETHER
WE WORK FOR THE COMPANY
THAT WORKS TO THE FUTURE
THEY WILL PROTECT US
WE WORK TOGETHER

I NEVER SEE YOU
WE ARE NEVER TOGETHER
I'LL LOVE YOU FOR EVER

I DRINK IN THE EVENINGS
IT HELPS WITH RELAXING
I CAN'T SLEEP WITHOUT DRINKING
WE DRINK TOGETHER
FROM MONDAY TO SATURDAY
I GO TO MY WORKPLACE
BUT ON SUNDAY WE ARE TOGETHER
YUKO AND HIRO

Tablature & Instructions Explained

The tablature stave comprises six lines, each representing a string on the guitar as illustrated.

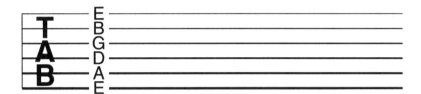

A number on any of the lines indicates, therefore, the string and fret on which a note should be played.

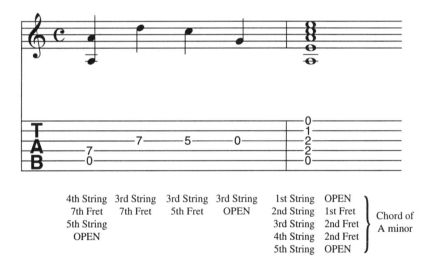

4th String	3rd String	3rd String	3rd String	1st String	OPEN	
7th Fret	7th Fret	5th Fret	OPEN	2nd String	1st Fret	Chord of
5th String				3rd String	2nd Fret	A minor
OPEN				4th String	2nd Fret	
				5th String	OPEN	

A useful hint to help you read tablature is to cut out small squares of self-adhesive paper and stick them on the upper edge of the guitar neck adjacent to each of the frets, numbering them accordingly. Be careful to use paper that will not damage the finish on your guitar.

Finger Vibrato

Tremolo Arm Vibrato

Glissando

Strike the note, then slide the finger up or down the fretboard as indicated.

Tremolo Strumming

This sign indicates fast up and down stroke strumming.

8va

This sign indicates that the notes are to be played an octave higher than written.

loco

This instruction cancels the above.

This note-head indicates the string is to be totally muted to produce a percussive effect.

P.M. = Palm mute

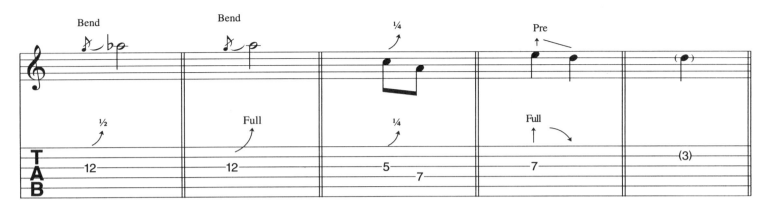

HALF TONE BEND

Play the note G then bend the string so that the pitch rises by a half tone (semi-tone).

FULL TONE BEND

DECORATIVE BEND

PRE-BEND

Bend the string as indicated, strike the string and release.

GHOST NOTE

The note is half sounded

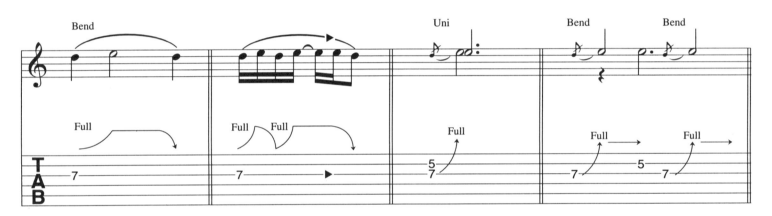

BEND & RELEASE

Strike the string, bend it as indicated, then release the bend whilst it is still sounding.

BEND & RESTRIKE

Strike the string, bend or gliss as indicated, then restrike the string where the symbol occurs.

UNISON BEND

Strike both strings simultaneously then immediately bend the lower string as indicated.

STAGGERED UNISON BEND

Strike the lower string and bend as indicated; whilst it is still sounding strike the higher string.

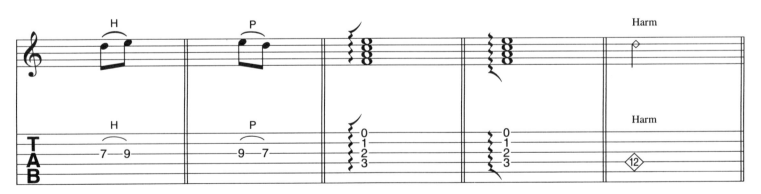

HAMMER-ON

Hammer a finger down on the next note without striking the string again.

PULL-OFF

Pull your finger off the string with a plucking motion to sound the next note without striking the string again.

RAKE-UP

Strum the notes upwards in the manner of an arpeggio.

RAKE-DOWN

Strum the notes downwards in the manner of an arpeggio.

HARMONICS

Strike the string whilst touching it lightly at the fret position shown. Artificial Harmonics, (A.H.), will be described in context.

Stereotypes

Words & Music by Damon Albarn, Graham Coxon, Alex James & David Rowntree

hus - band said good - bye. She wears a low cut T - shirt, runs a lit - tle B and B, she's

Let ring…

most ac - com - mo - dat - ing when she's in her lin - ger - ie. Wife

swap - ping is your fu - ture, you know that it would suit you.

etc.

⊓ = downstroke

Chorus:

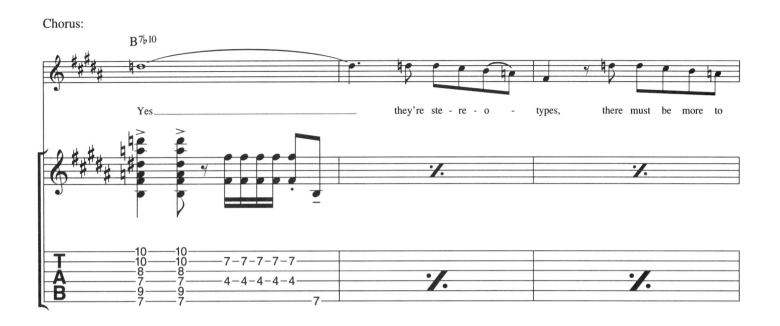

Yes_____ they're ste - re - o - types, there must be more to

life. All your life you're___ dream - ing,___ then you stop dream - ing. From

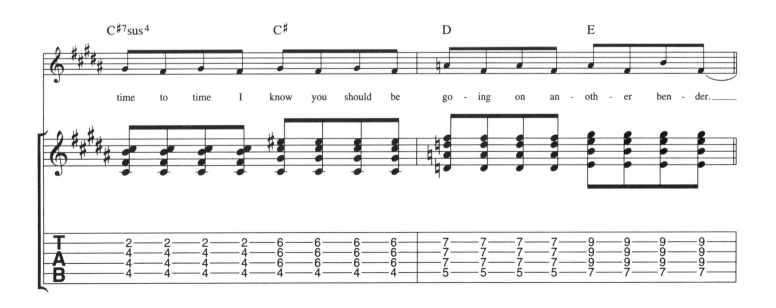

time to time I know you should be go - ing on an - oth - er ben - der.___

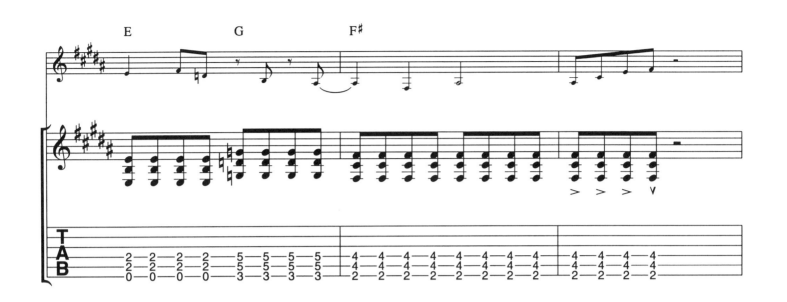

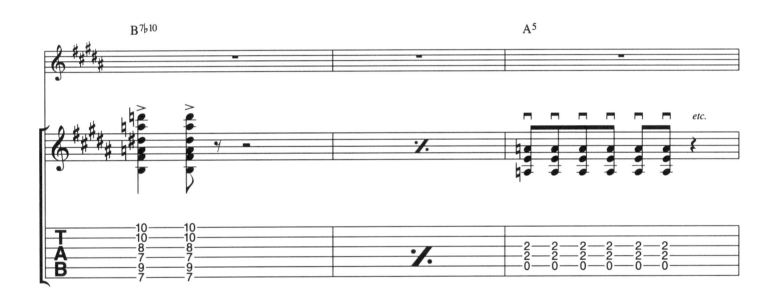

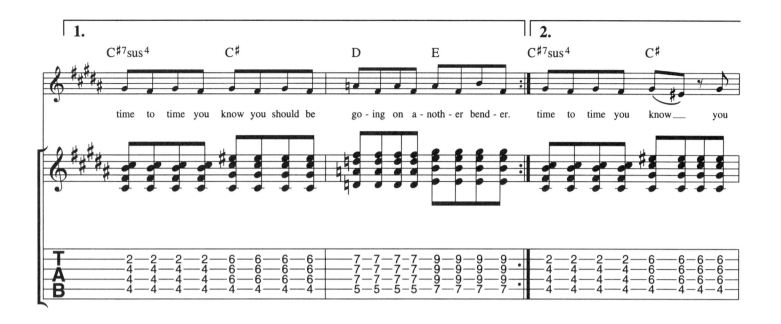

time to time you know you should be go-ing on a-noth-er bend-er. time to time you know___ you

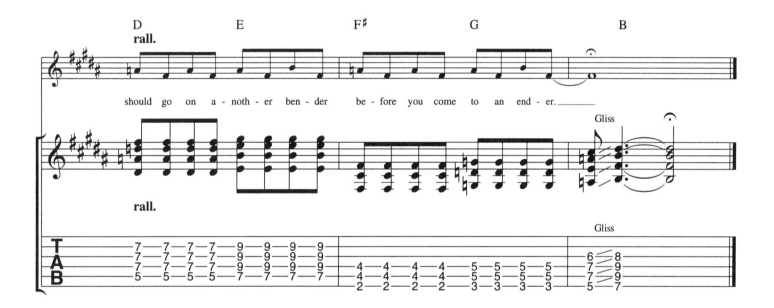

should go on a-noth-er ben-der be-fore you come to an end-er.____

Verse 2:
The suburbs they are sleeping but he's dressing up tonight
She likes a man in uniform, he likes to wear it tight
They're on the lover's sofa, they're on the patio
And when the fun is over, watch themselves on video.

The neighbours may be staring
But they are just past caring.

Country House

Words & Music by Damon Albarn, Graham Coxon, Alex James & David Rowntree

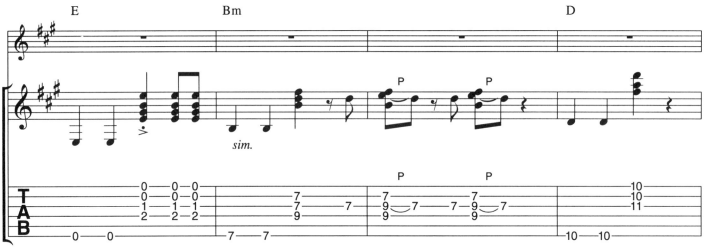

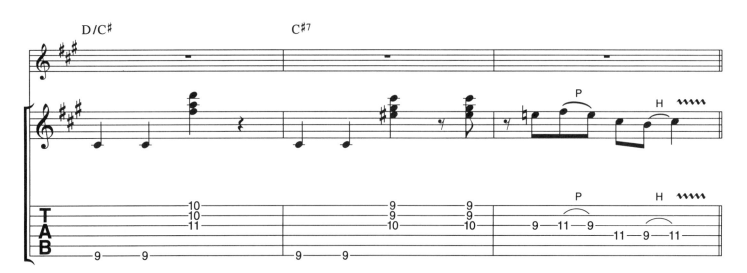

Verse:

1. Ci - ty dwel - ler suc - cess - ful fel - ler, thought to him - self "Oops, I've got a lot of mon - ey,___

See Block Lyrics for Verse 2

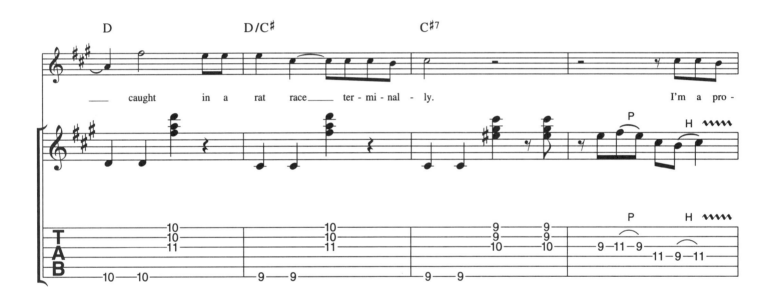

___ caught in a rat race___ ter - mi - nal - ly. I'm a pro -

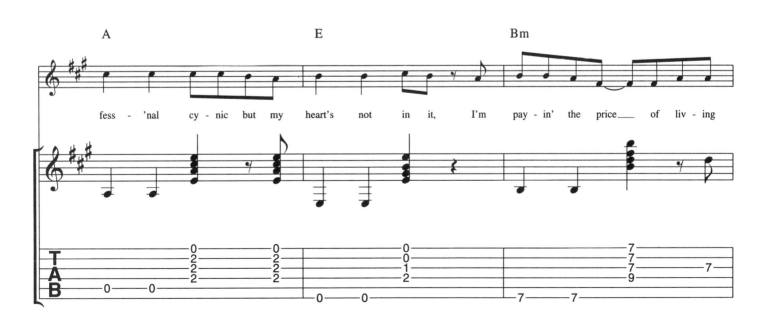

fess - 'nal cy - nic but my heart's not in it, I'm pay - in' the price___ of liv - ing

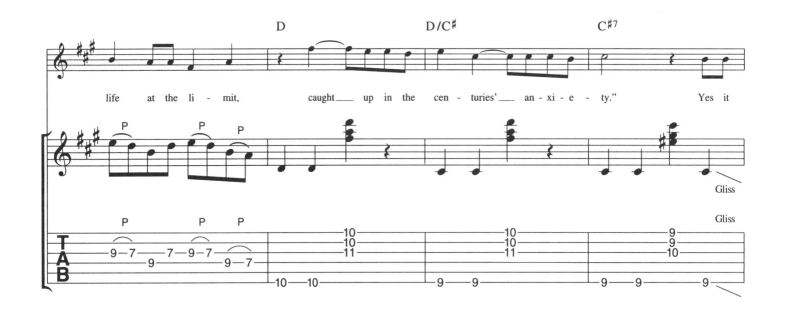

life at the li - mit, caught___ up in the cen - turies'___ an - xi - e - ty." Yes it

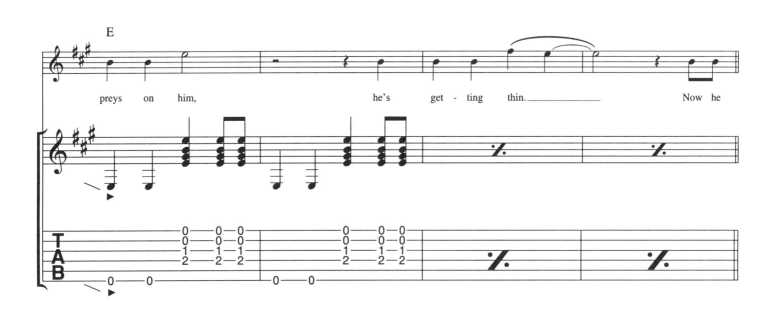

preys on him, he's get - ting thin._____ Now he

Chorus:

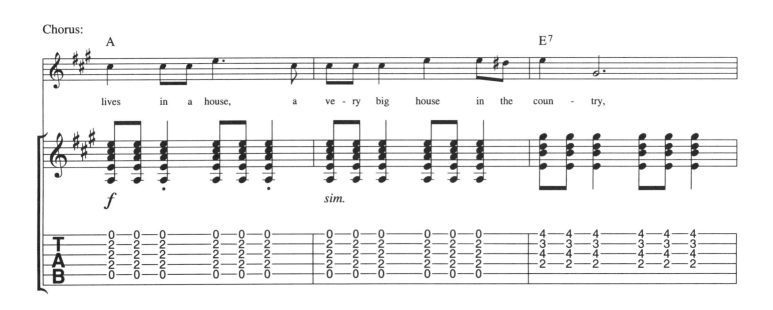

lives in a house, a ve - ry big house in the coun - try,

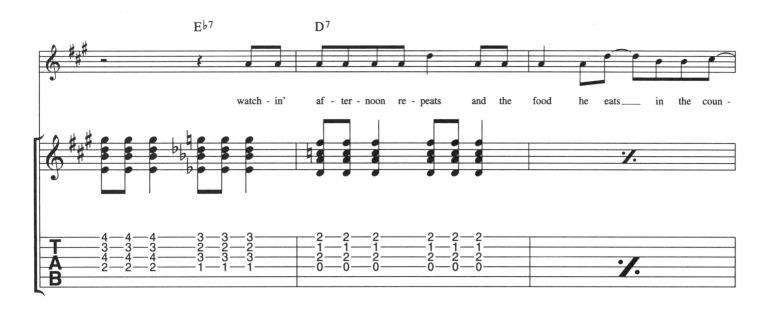

watch - in' af - ter - noon re - peats and the food he eats___ in the coun -

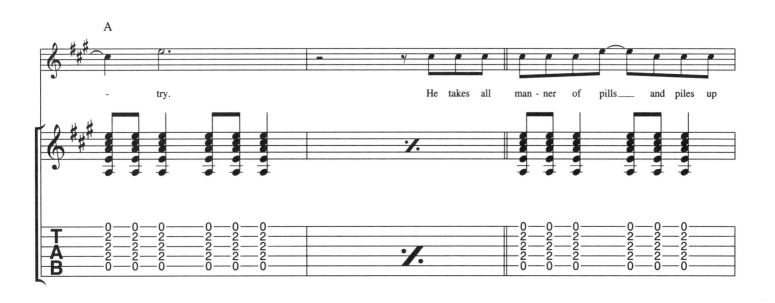

- try.   He takes all man - ner of pills___ and piles up

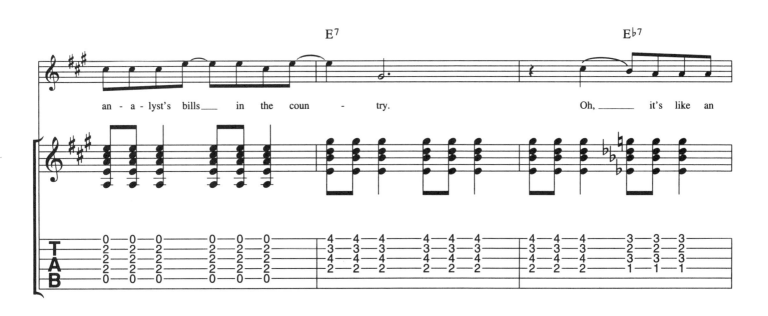

an - a - lyst's bills___ in the coun - - try.   Oh, ___ it's like an

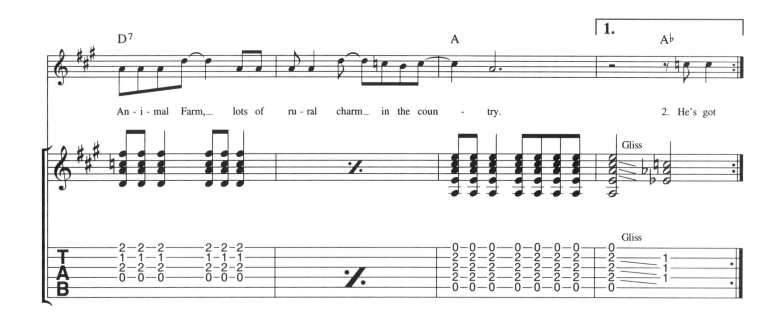

An - i - mal Farm,__ lots of ru - ral charm__ in the coun - try.   2. He's got

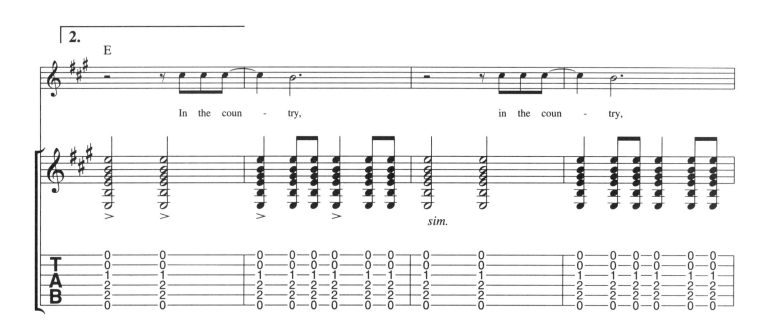

In the coun - try,   in the coun - try,

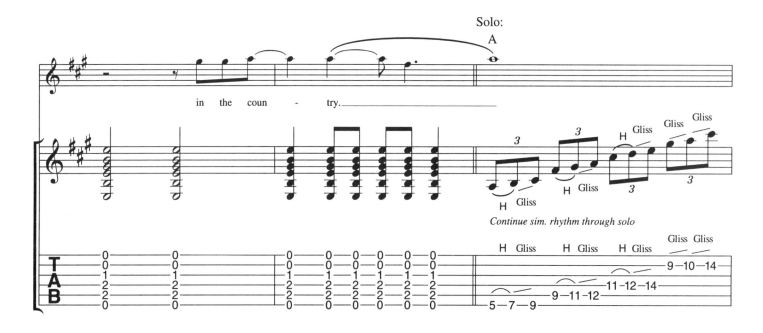

in the coun - try._____

Continue sim. rhythm through solo

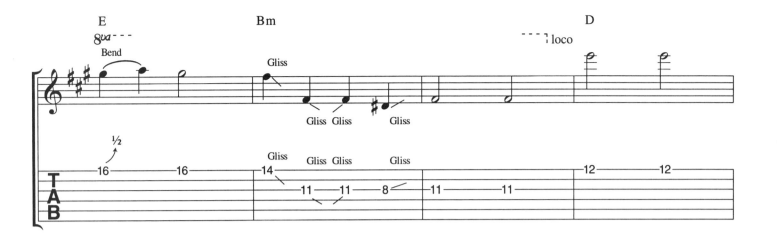

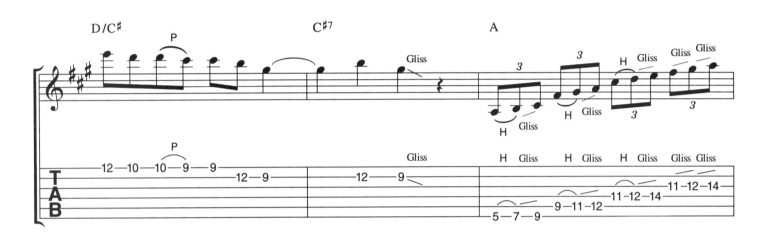

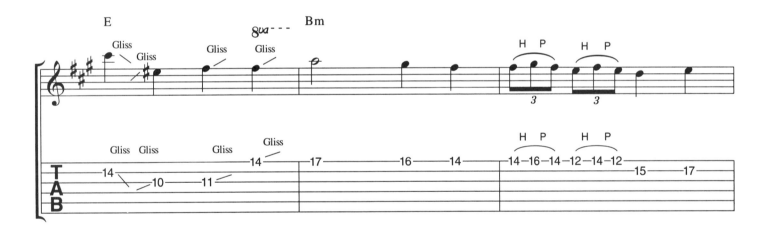

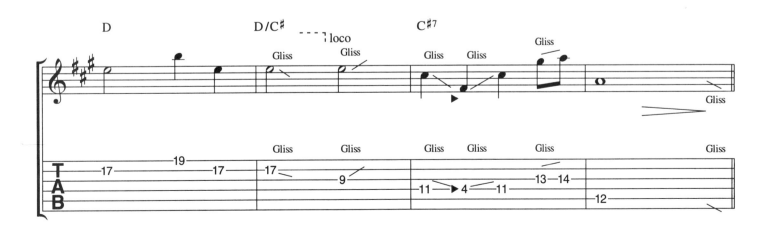

Bridge:

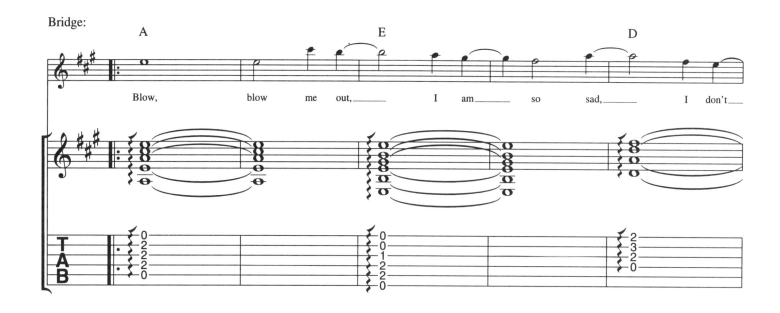

Blow, blow me out,_____ I am_____ so sad,_____ I don't

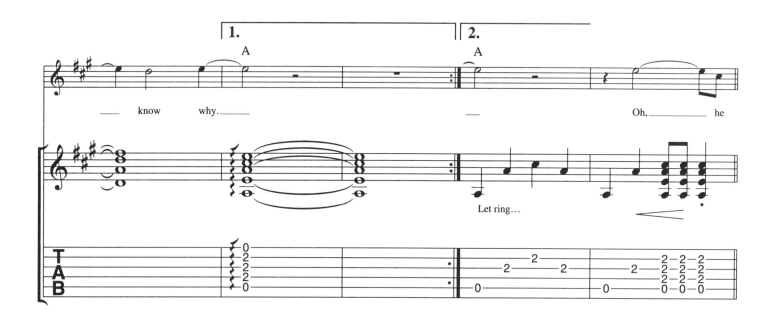

— know why._____ — Oh,_____ he

Let ring…

Chorus:

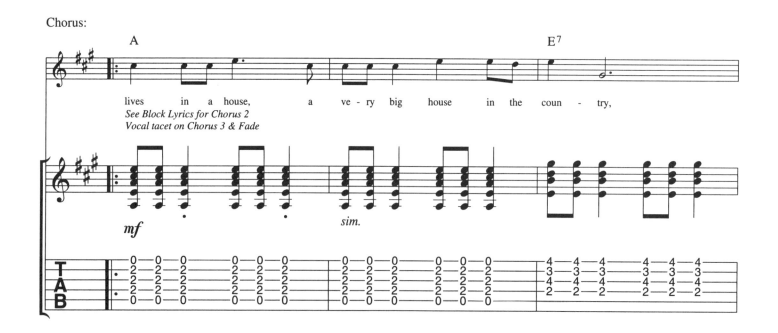

lives in a house, a ve - ry big house in the coun - try,

See Block Lyrics for Chorus 2
Vocal tacet on Chorus 3 & Fade

mf   *sim.*

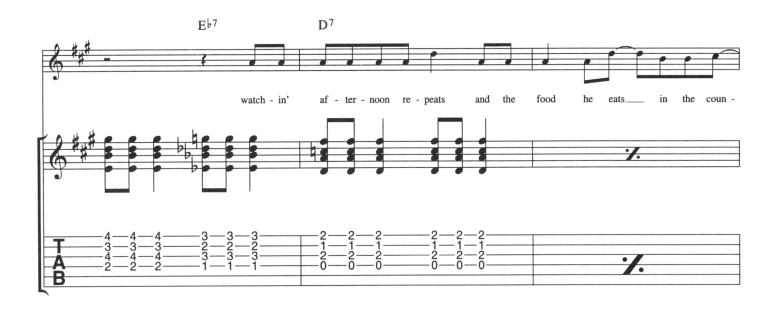

watch-in' af-ter-noon re-peats and the food he eats___ in the coun-

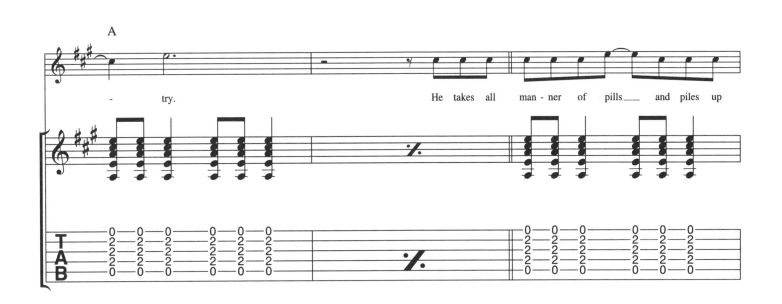

-try. He takes all man-ner of pills___ and piles up

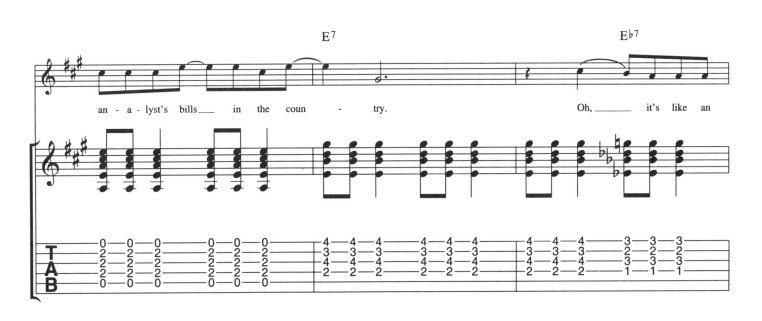

an-a-lyst's bills___ in the coun - try. Oh, ___ it's like an

an - i - mal farm,___ lots of ru - ral charm___ in the coun - try.

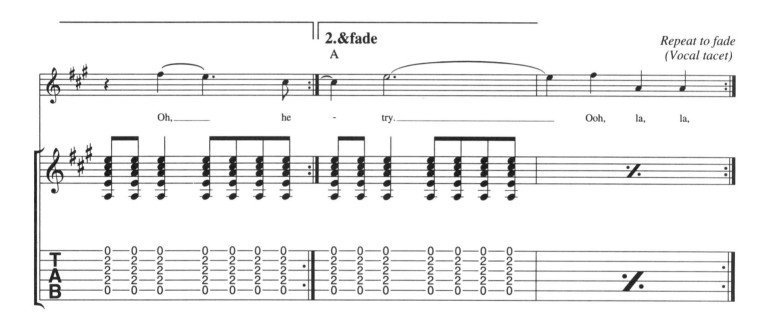

Oh,_____ he - try._____ Ooh, la, la,

Repeat to fade
(Vocal tacet)

Verse 2:
He's got morning glory
And life's a different story
Everything's going Jackanory
In touch with his own mortality
He's reading Balzac, knocking back Prozac
It's a helping hand that makes you feel wonderfully bland
Oh, it's the century's remedy
For the faint at heart, a new start.

Chorus 2:
He lives in a house, a very big house in the country
He's got a fog in his chest
So he needs a lot of rest in the country
He doesn't drink, smoke, laugh
Takes herbal baths in the country
But you'll come to no harm on the animal farm in the country.

Charmless Man

Words & Music by Damon Albarn, Graham Coxon, Alex James & David Rowntree

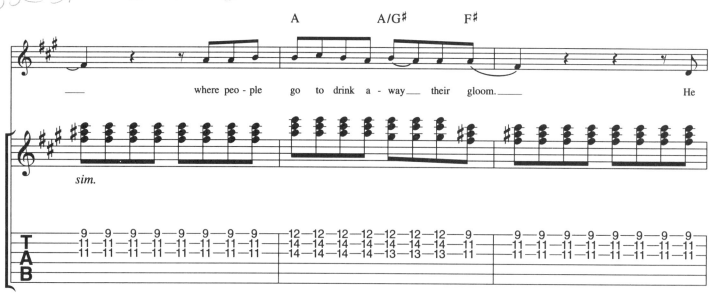

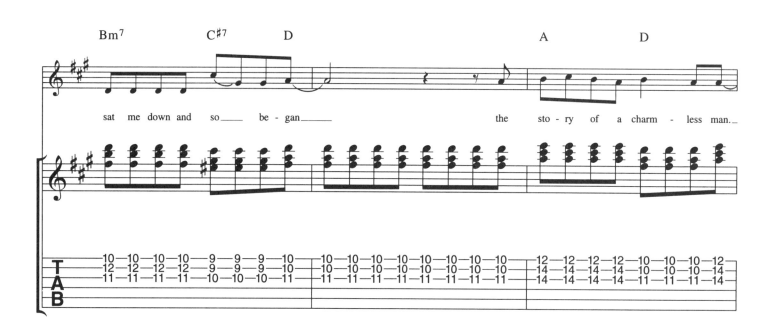

See Block Lyrics for Verse 3

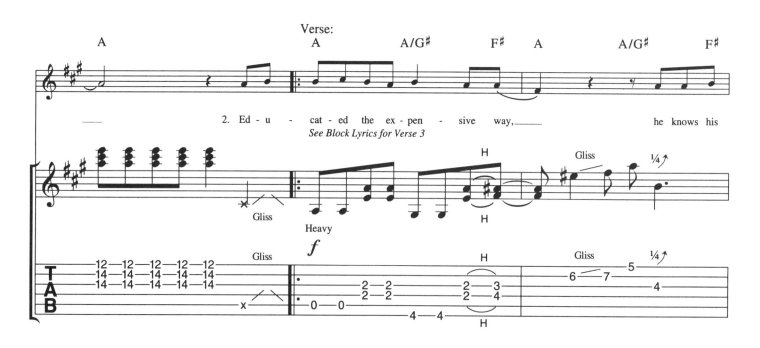

Cla - ret from his Beau - jol - ais._____ I think he'd like to have been Ron - nie Kray,__

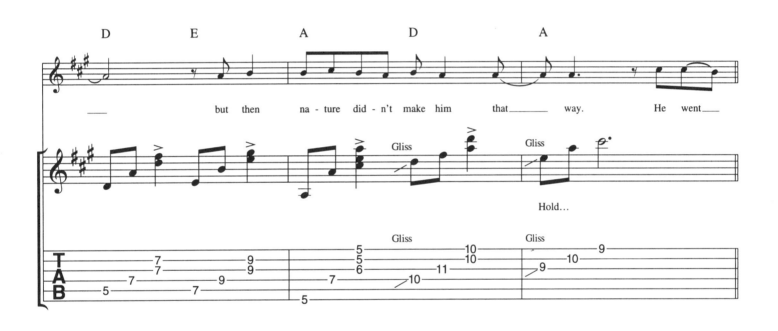

_____ but then na - ture did - n't make him that_____ way. He went__

Chorus:

na na na na na na na,_____ na na na na na na na na na.__

See Block Lyrics for Chorus 2:

He thinks his ed - u - ca - ted airs,_____ those fam - 'ly shares_

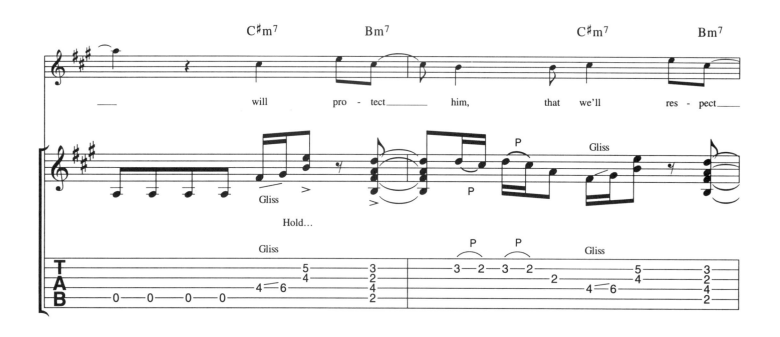

_____ will pro - tect_____ him, that we'll res - pect_____

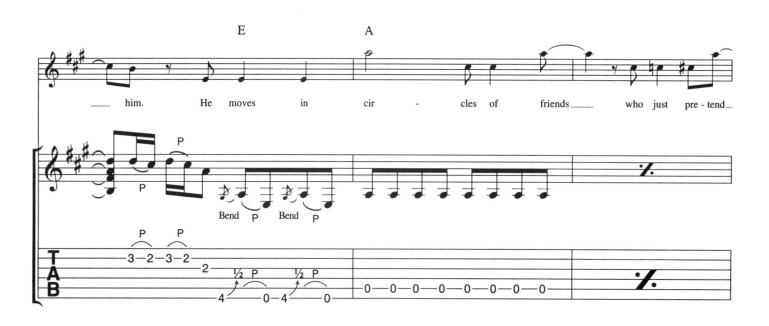

_____ him. He moves in cir - cles of friends_____ who just pre - tend_

28

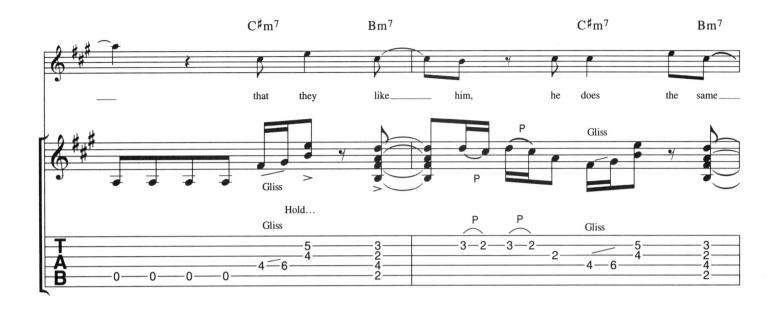

that they like_____ him, he does the same_____

_____ to them_____ and when you put it all to-geth-er there's the mo-del of a charm-less man.__

Na na na na na na na,_____ na na na na na na na na.__

3. He knows the

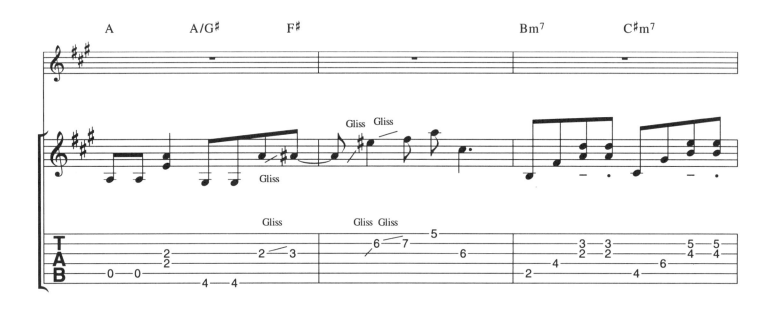

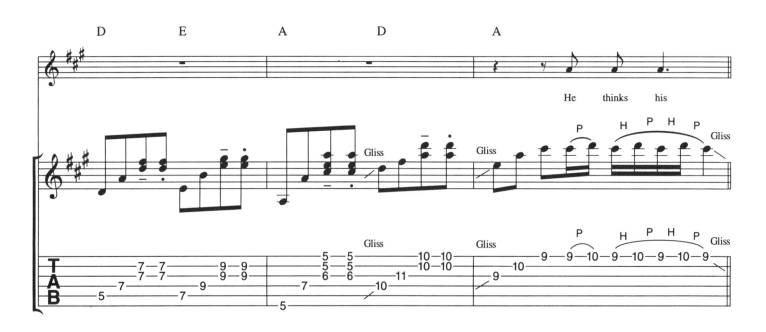

He thinks his

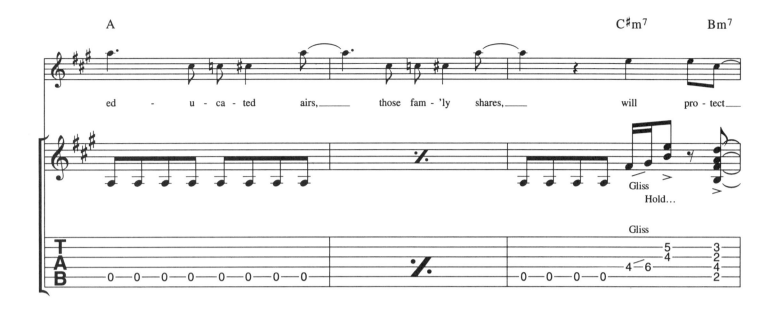

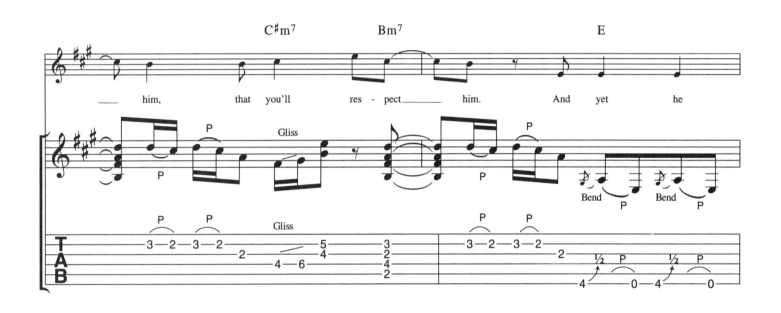

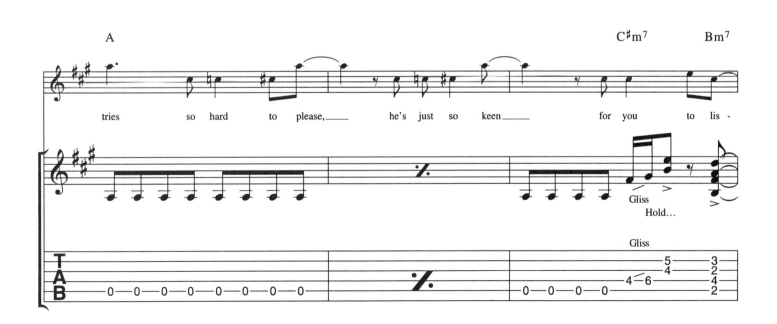

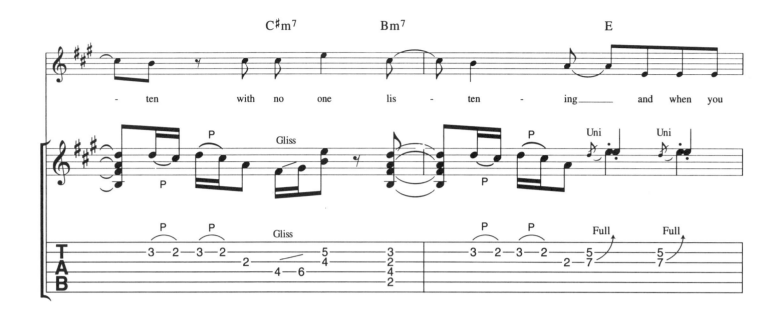

- ten with no one lis - ten - ing_____ and when you

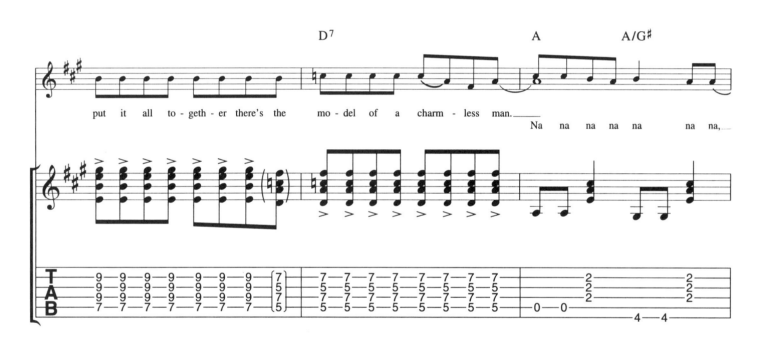

put it all to - geth - er there's the mo - del of a charm - less man._____ Na na na na na na na,_____

na na na na na na na na,_____ na na

32

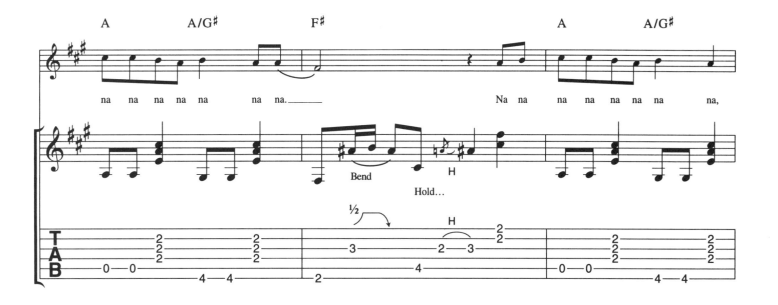

Verse 3:
He knows the swingers and their cavalry
Says he can get in anywhere for free
I began to go a little cross-eyed
And from this charmless man I just had to hide.

Chorus 2:
He went na na na na na na na
Na na na na na na na na na
He talks at speed, he gets nose bleeds
He doesn't see his days
Are tumbling down upon him
And yet he tries so hard to please
He's just so keen for you to listen
But no one is listening
And when you put it all together
There's the model of a charmless man.

Best Days

Words & Music by Damon Albarn, Graham Coxon, Alex James & David Rowntree

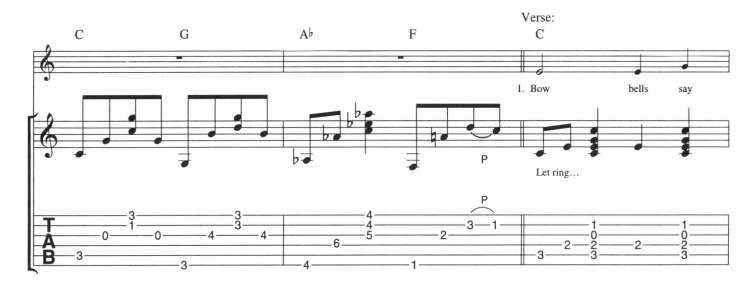

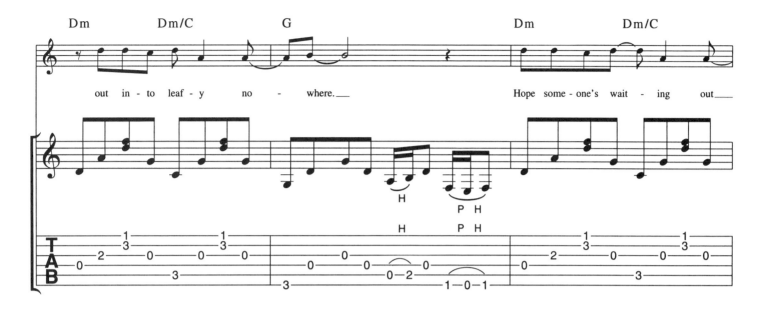

out in-to leaf-y no - where.___   Hope some-one's wait - ing out___

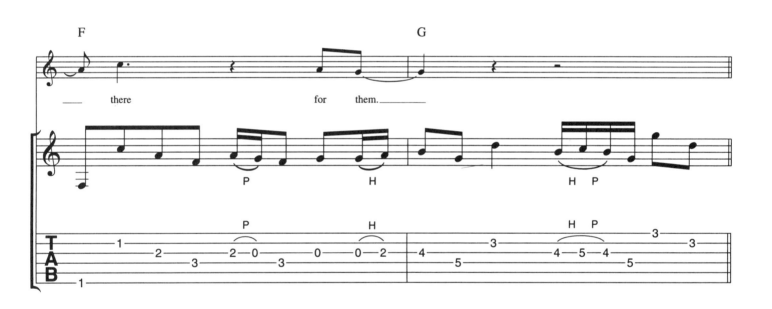

___ there   for them._____

Verse:

𝄋 C   Am   C

2. Cab - bie has his mind on a fare___ to the sun,___   he works

See Block Lyrics for Verse 3(𝄋)

35

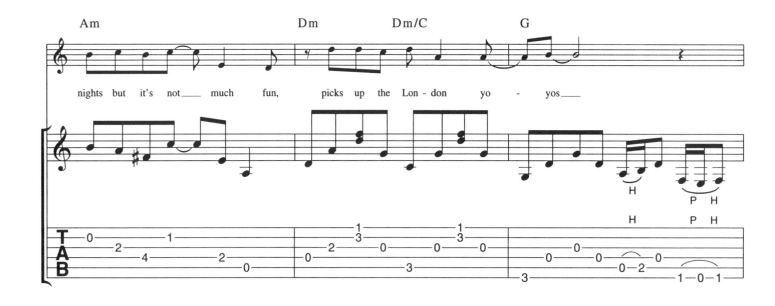

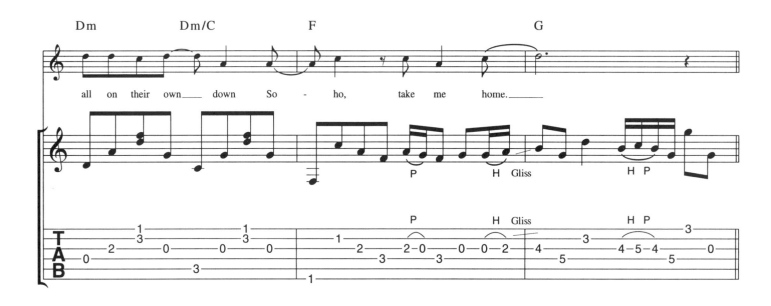

Chorus:

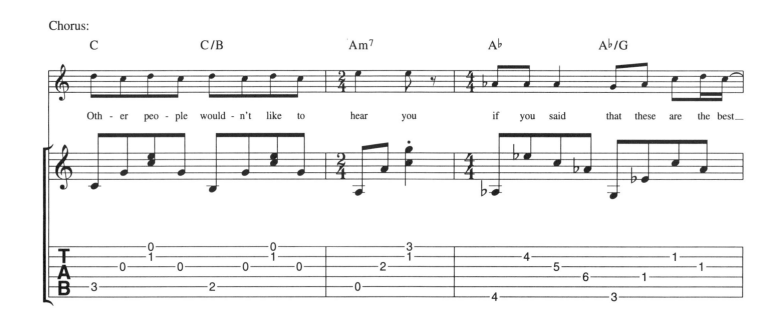

days   of   our   lives.   Oth - er   peo - ple   turn a - round___ and   laugh   at   you

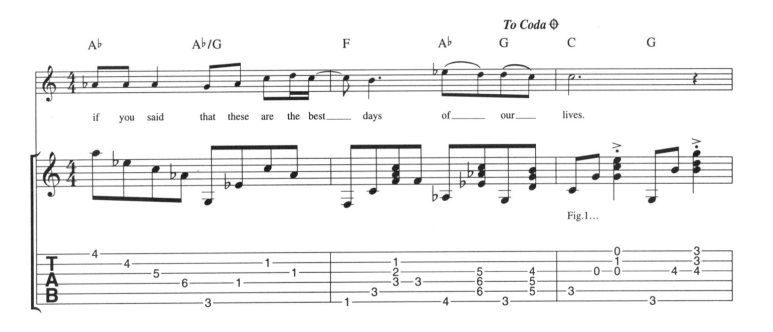

if   you   said   that   these   are   the   best___   days   of___   our___   lives.

Fig.1...

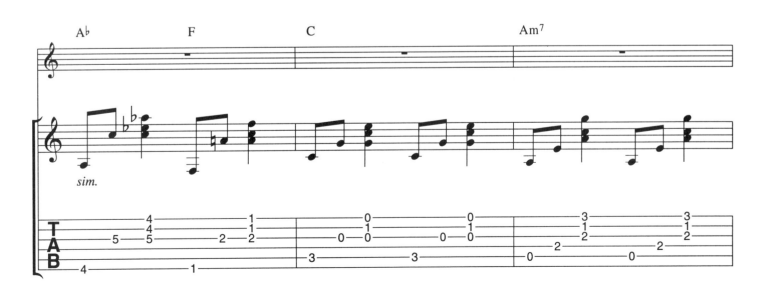

sim.

Trel - lick. Tower's____ been call -

- ing,_____ I know_____ she'll leave____ me in the

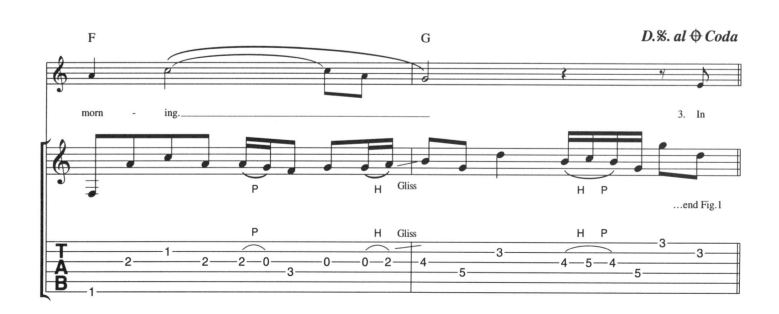

morn - ing._____ 3. In

...end Fig.1

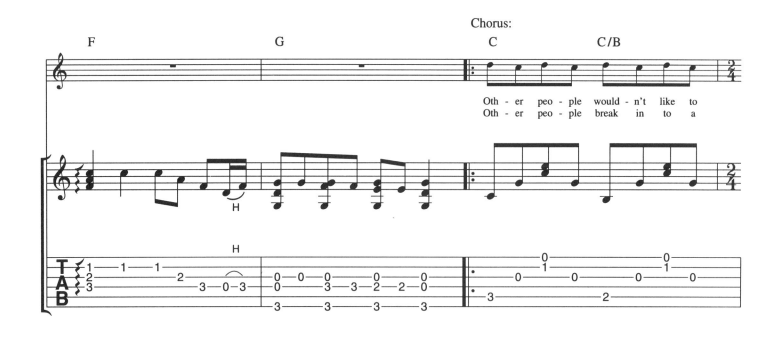

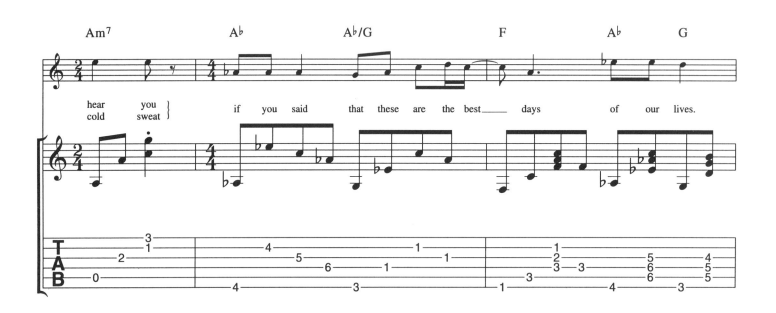

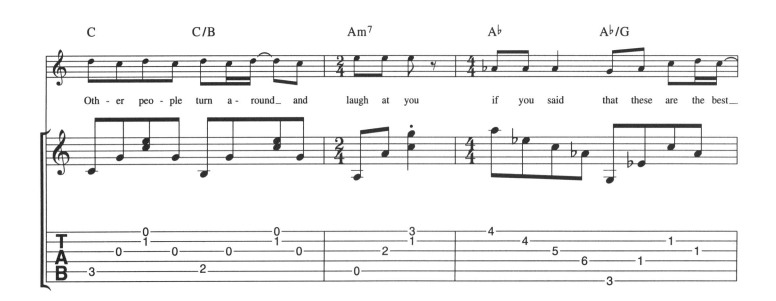

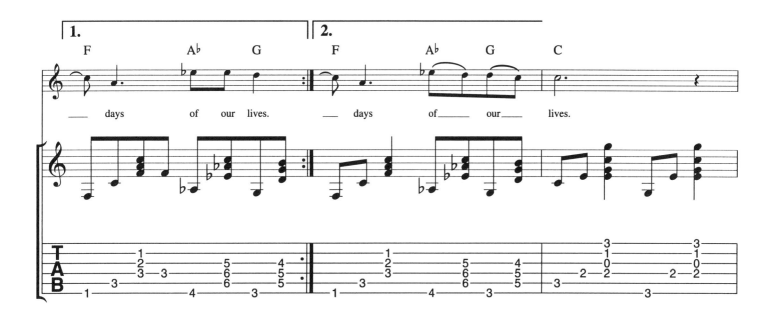

days of our lives. days of our lives.

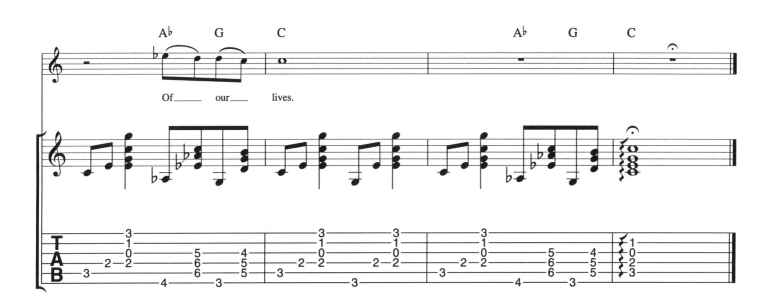

Of our lives.

Verse 3:
In hotel cells listening to dull tones
Remote controls and cable moans
In his drink he's talking
Gets disconnected sleep-walking back home.

Top Man

Words & Music by Damon Albarn, Graham Coxon, Alex James & David Rowntree

Verse:

is a pub - lic warn - ing, be care - ful when you're out, we're

See Block Lyrics for Verse 3

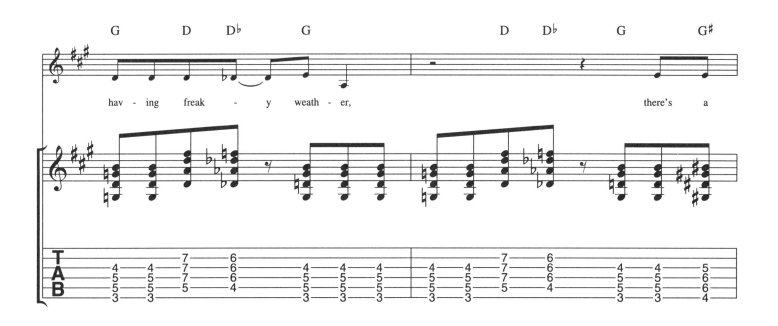

hav - ing freak - y weath - er, there's a

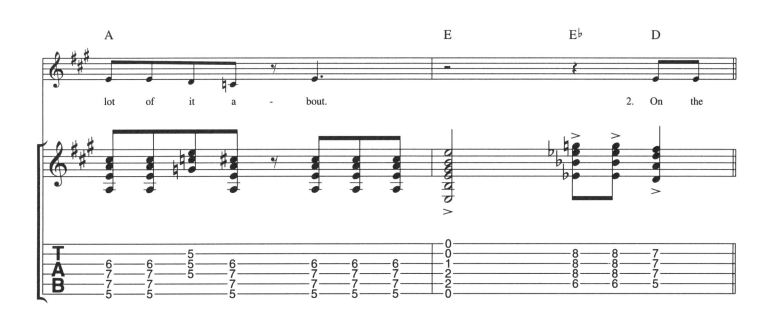

lot of it a - bout. 2. On the

44

45

46

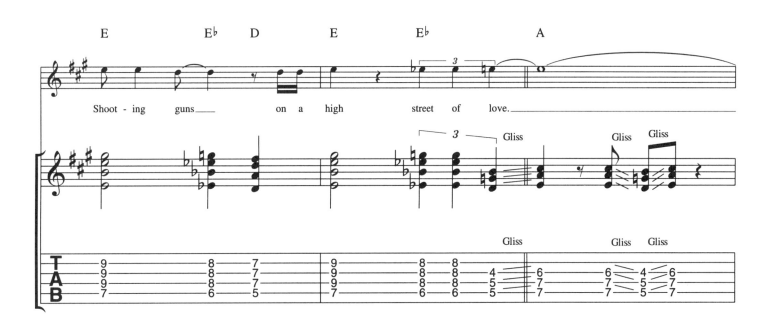

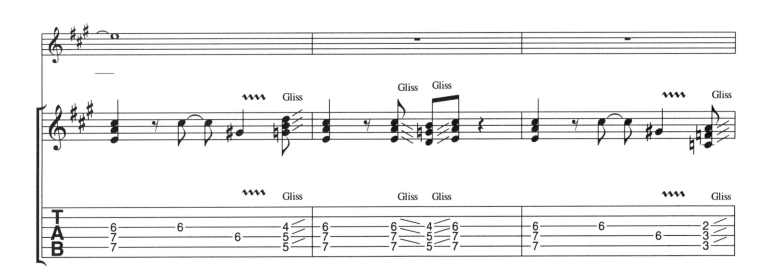

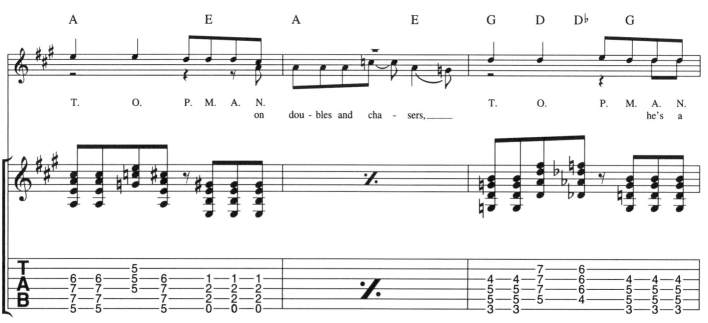

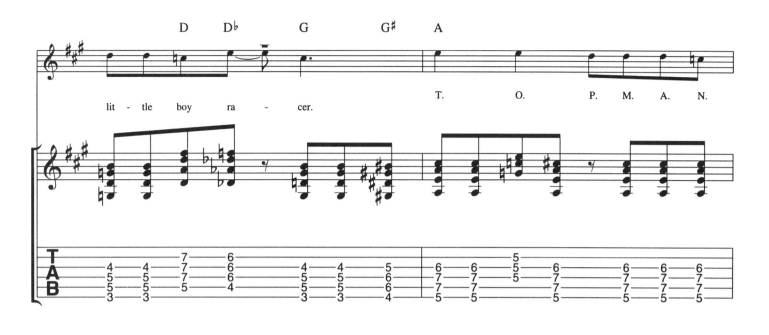

little boy ra - cer.

T. O. P. M. A. N.

Shoot - ing guns in the high streets of_____ love.

T. O. P. M. A. N.

Repeat to fade

Verse 3:
In a crowd it's hard to spot him
But anonymity can cost
It's never cheap or cheerful
He's Hugo and he's Boss.

Verse 4:
He's riding through the desert
On a camel light
And on a magic carpet
He'll fly away tonight.

Fade Away

Words & Music by Damon Albarn, Graham Coxon, Alex James & David Rowntree

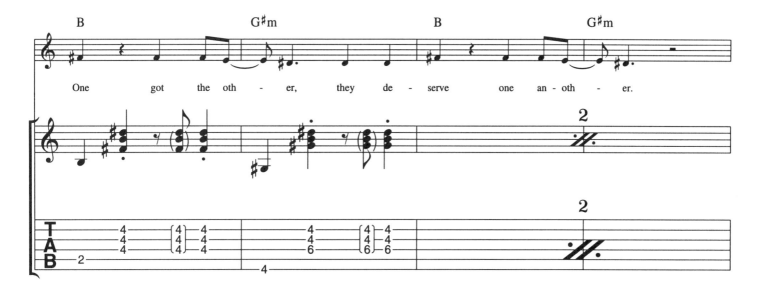

One got the oth - er, they de - serve one an - oth - er.

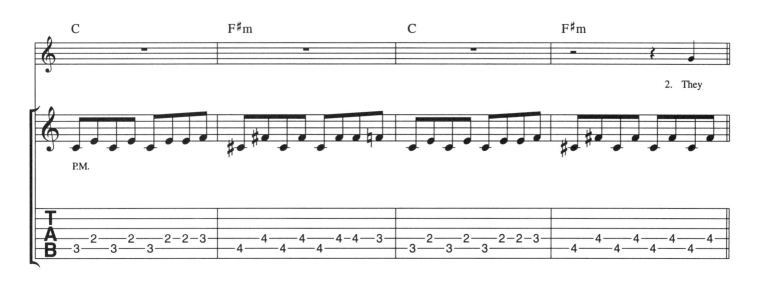

2. They

P.M.

set - tled in a brand new town, with

See Block Lyrics for Verse 3

P.M.

51

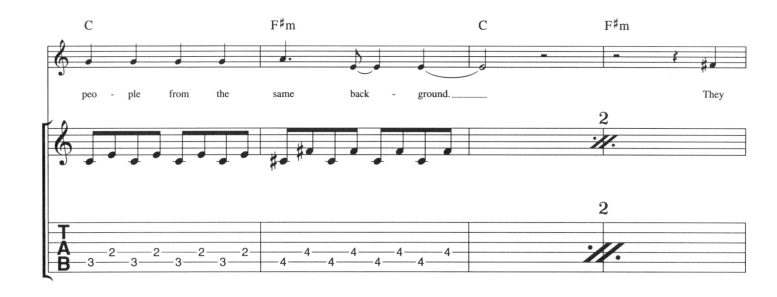

peo - ple from the same back - ground._____ They

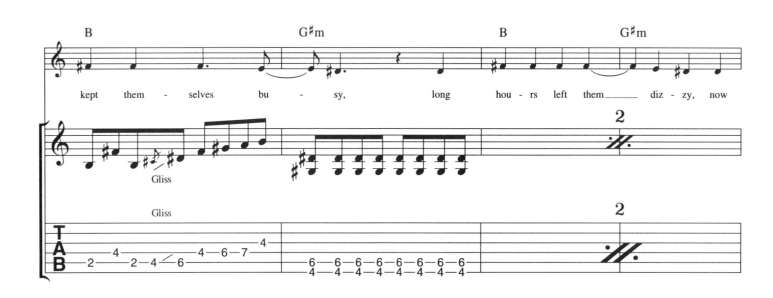

kept them - selves bu - sy, long hou - rs left them_____ diz - zy, now

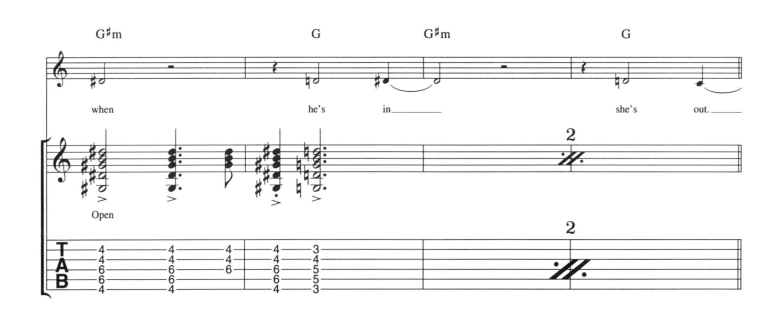

when he's in_____ she's out._____

52

Chorus:

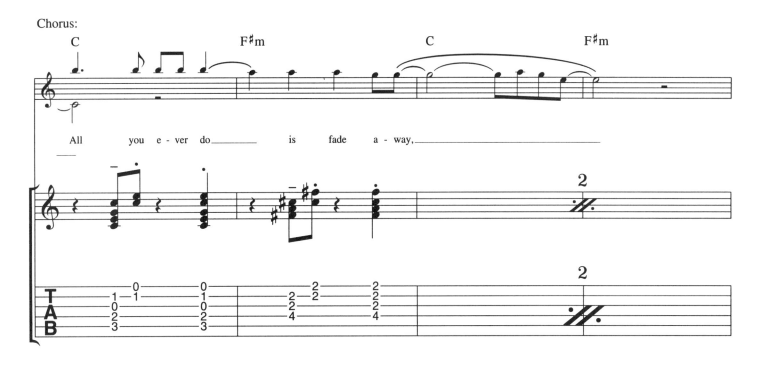

All you e - ver do_____ is fade a - way,_____

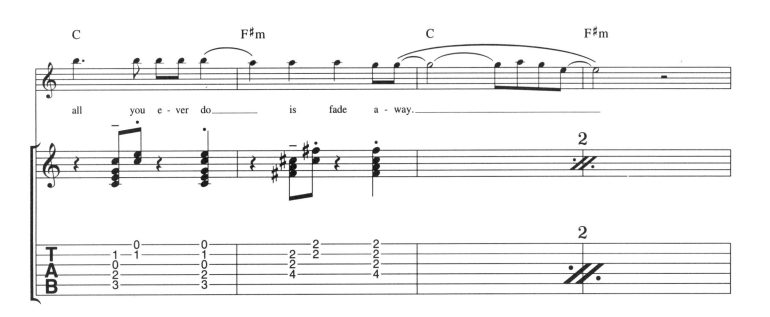

all you e - ver do_____ is fade a - way._____

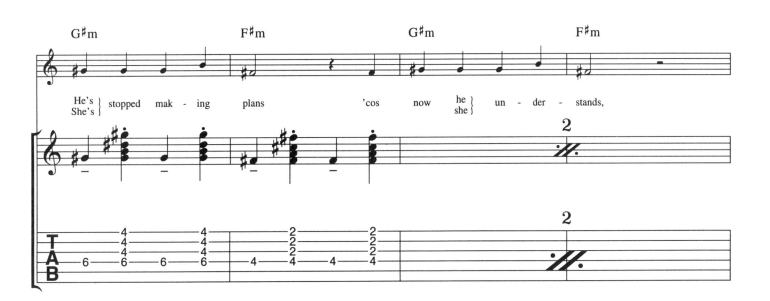

He's } stopped mak - ing plans 'cos now he } un - der - stands,
She's } she }

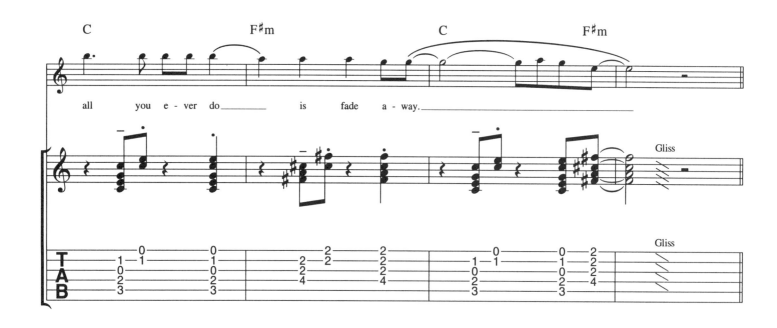

all you e - ver do_____ is fade a - way._____

out. (𝄋 only)

P.M.

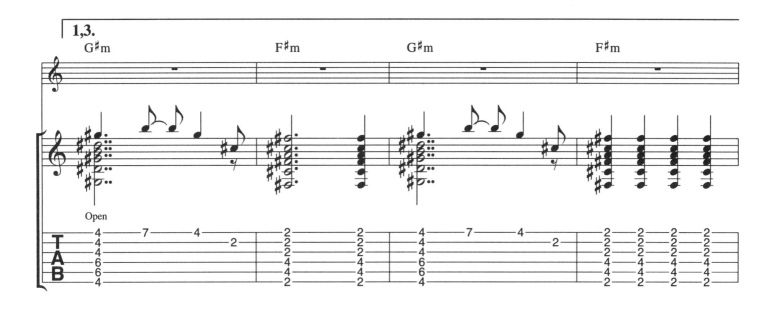

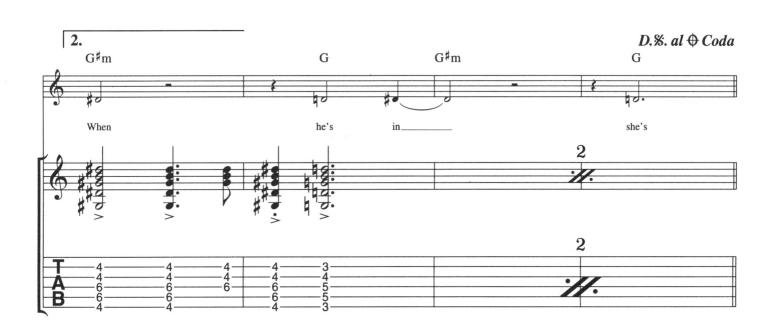

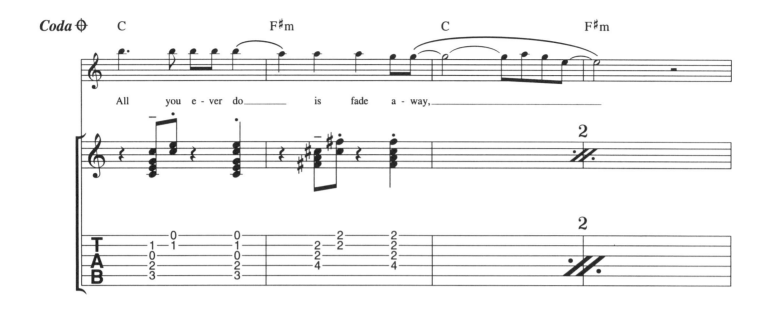

Coda ⊕

All you e-ver do___ is fade a-way,_____

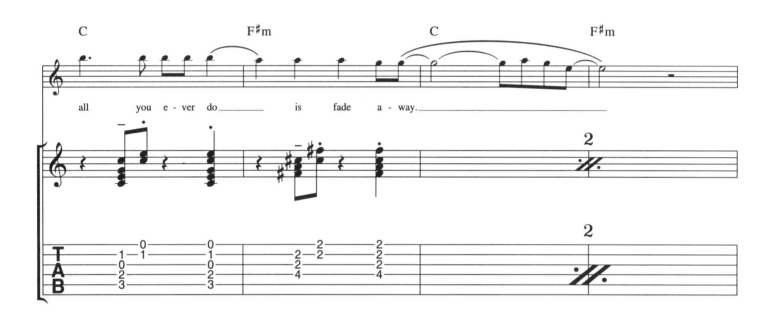

all you e-ver do___ is fade a - way._____

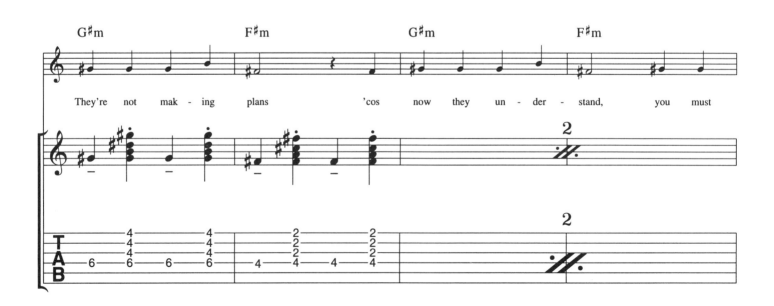

They're not mak - ing plans 'cos now they un - der - stand, you must

learn to for - get,_____ 'cos this is all you'll e - ver get._____

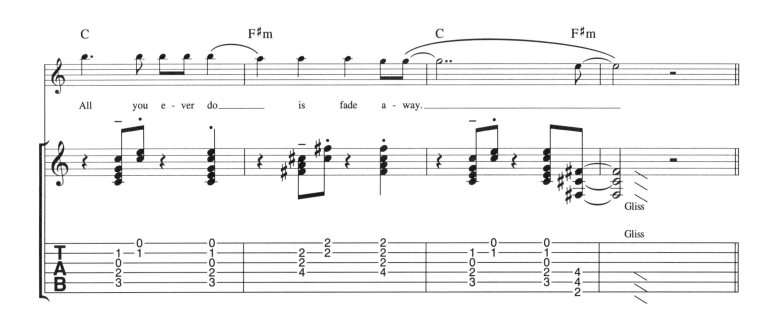

All you e - ver do_____ is fade a - way._____

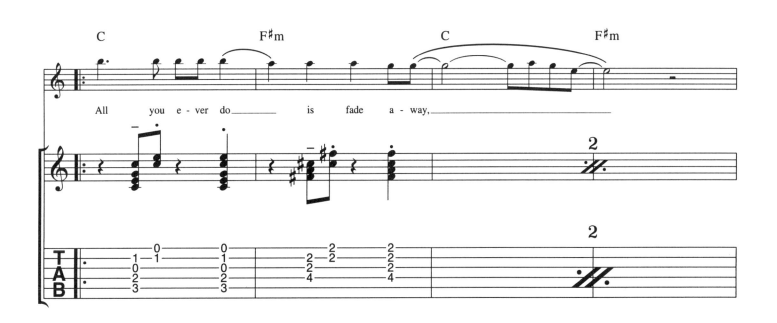

All you e - ver do_____ is fade a - way,_____

Verse 3:
He noticed he had visible lines
She worried about her behind
Their birth had been the death of them
It didn't really bother them
Now when she's in, he's out.

The Universal

Words & Music by Damon Albarn, Graham Coxon, Alex James & David Rowntree

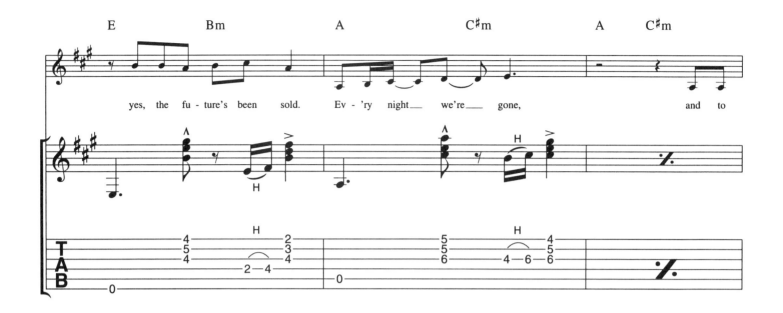

yes, the fu-ture's been sold. Ev-'ry night___ we're___ gone, and to

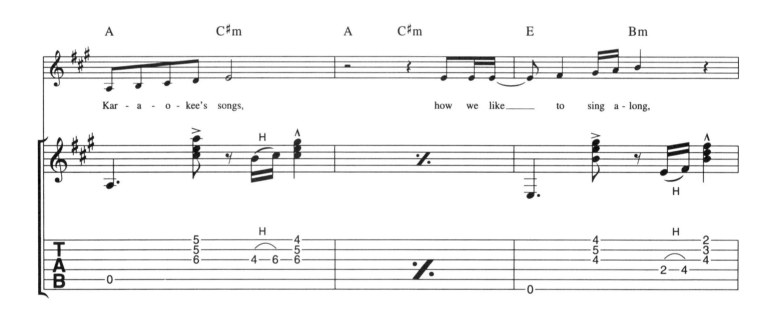

Kar - a - o - kee's songs, how we like_____ to sing a - long,

Chorus:

though the words are wrong. It real - ly, real - ly, real - ly could hap - pen, yes it real-

= downstroke

60

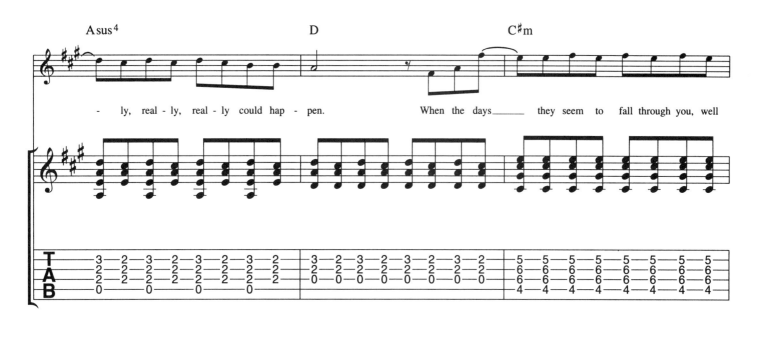

- ly, real - ly, real - ly could hap - pen. When the days_____ they seem to fall through you, well

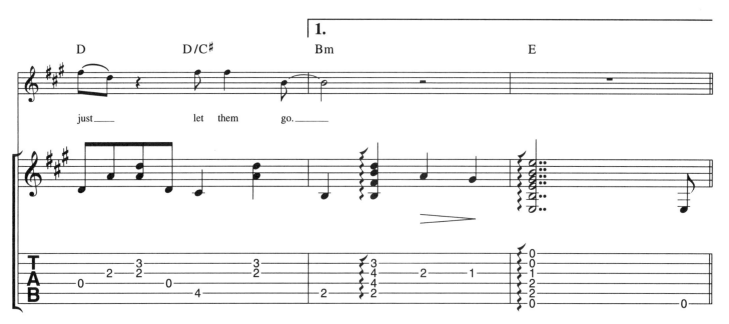

just____ let them go.____

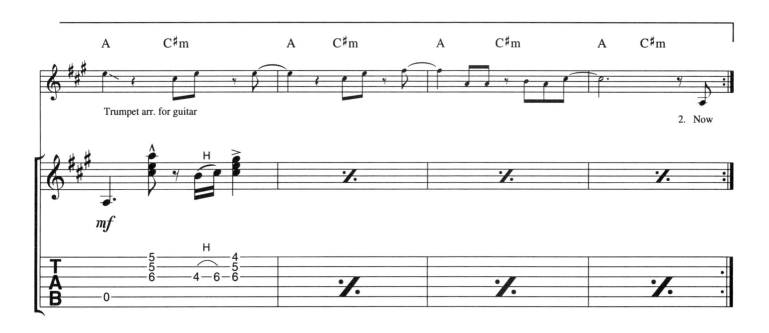

Trumpet arr. for guitar

2. Now

mf

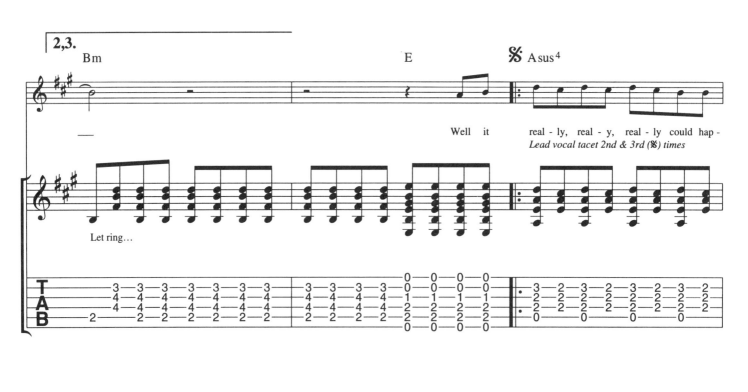

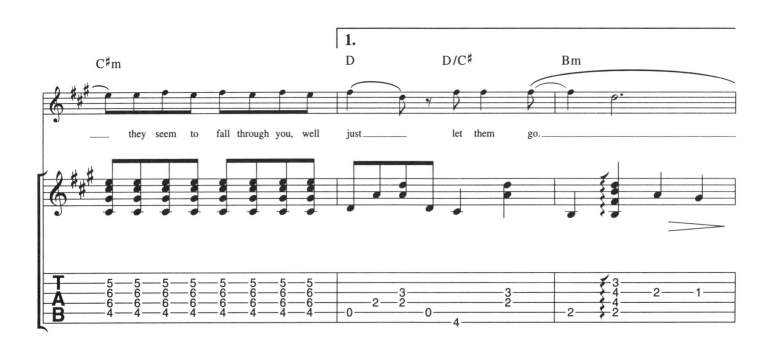

Verse 2:
No one here is alone
Satellites in every home
Yes, the Universal's here
Here for everyone.

Every paper that you read
Says tomorrow's your lucky day
Well, here's your lucky day.

Mr. Robinson's Quango

Words & Music by Damon Albarn, Graham Coxon, Alex James & David Rowntree

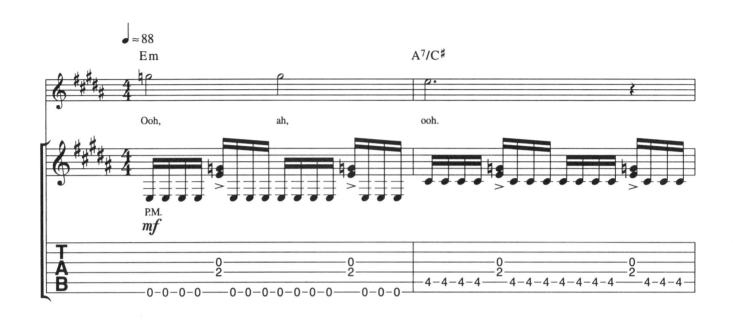

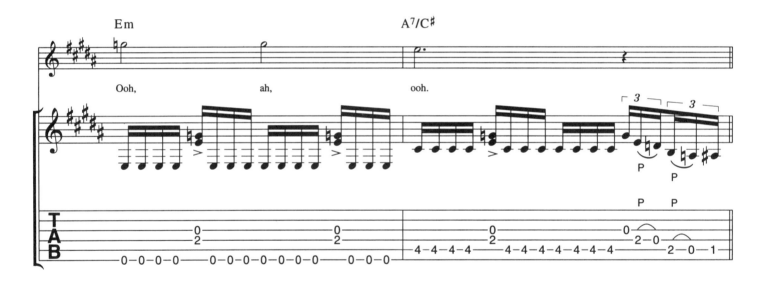

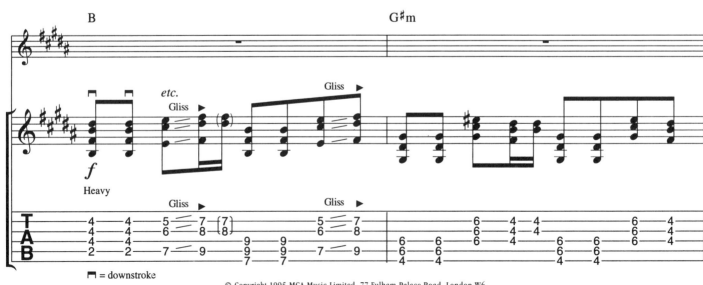

Verse:

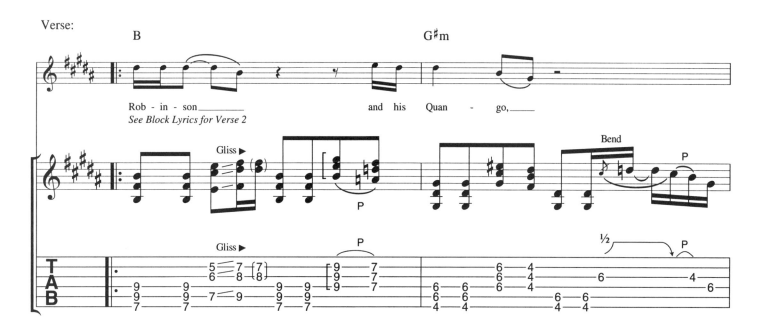

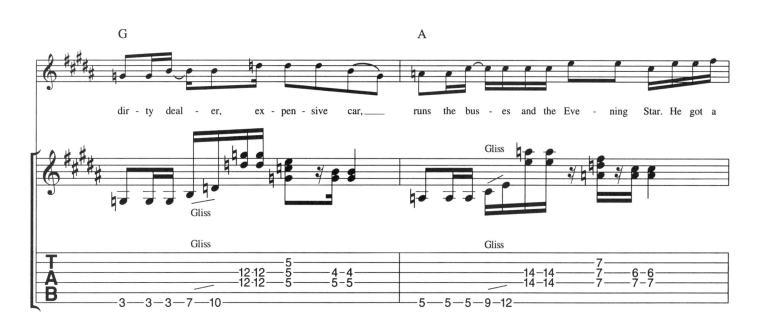

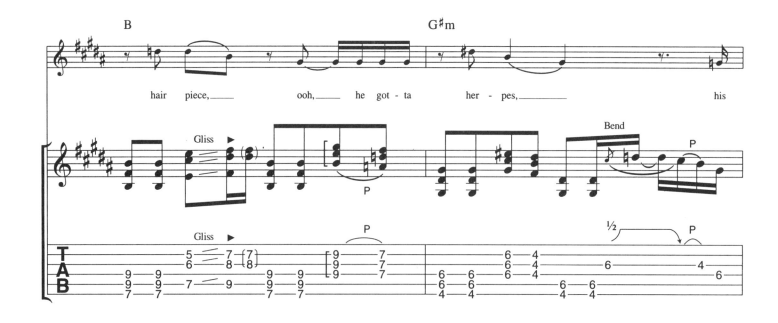

hair piece,_____ ooh,_____ he got - ta her - pes,_____ his

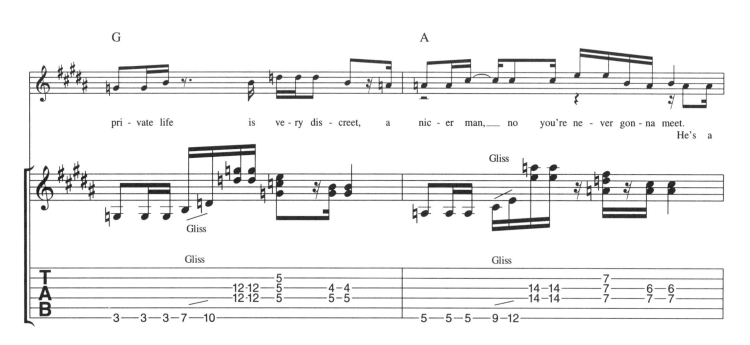

pri - vate life is ve - ry dis - creet, a nic - er man,___ no you're ne - ver gon - na meet. He's a

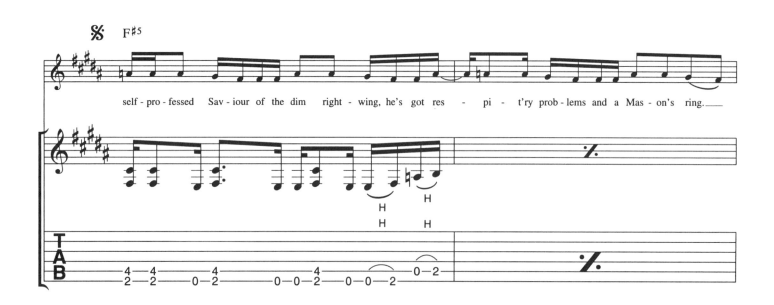

self - pro - fessed Sav - iour of the dim right - wing, he's got res - - pi - t'ry prob - lems and a Mas - on's ring.___

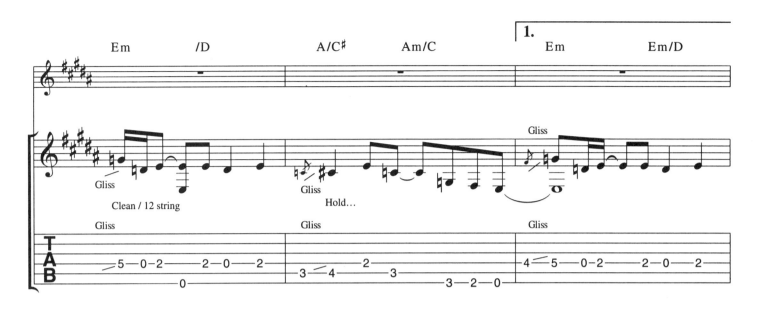

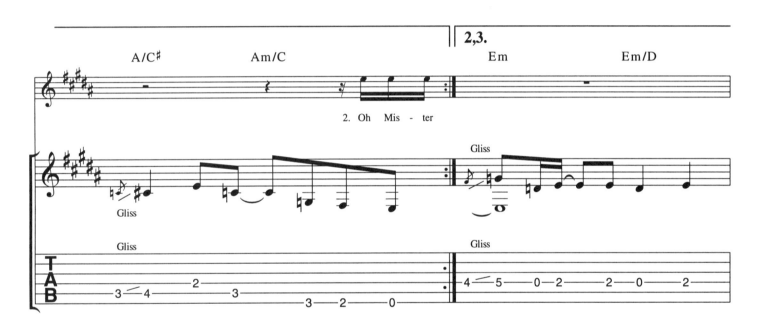

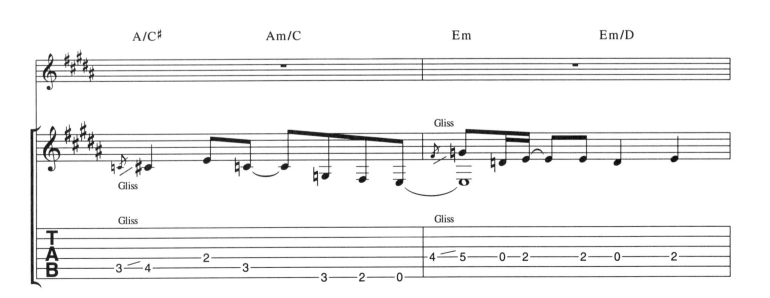

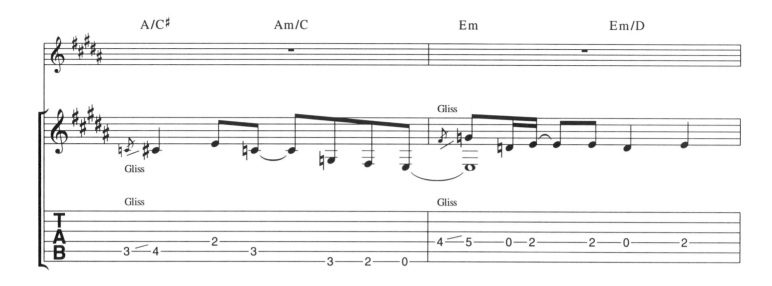

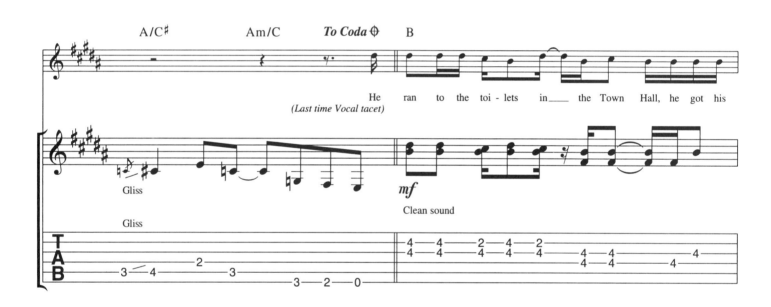

He ran to the toi - lets in____ the Town Hall, he got his

bi - ro out and he wrote____ on the wall: "I'm wear - ing

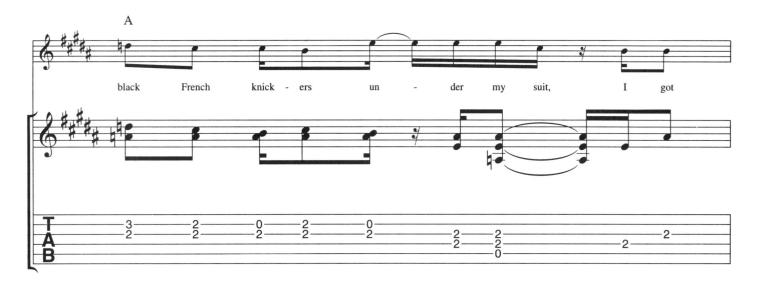

black French knick - ers un - der my suit, I got

stock - ings and sus - pen - ders and I'm real - ly ra - ther loose. _____

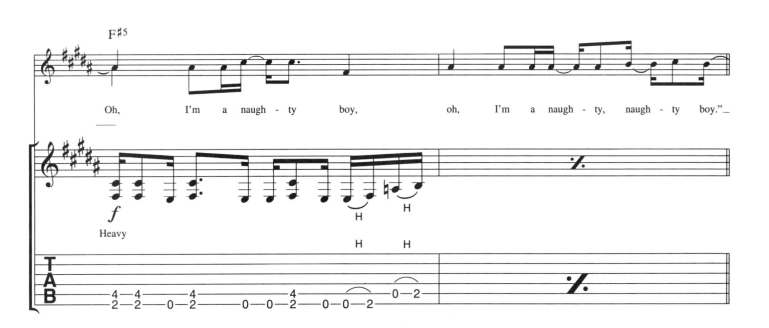

Oh, I'm a naugh - ty boy, oh, I'm a naugh - ty, naugh - ty boy." _

(1st time only) I   said   "Ooh".____

⊓ = downstroke
∨ = upstroke

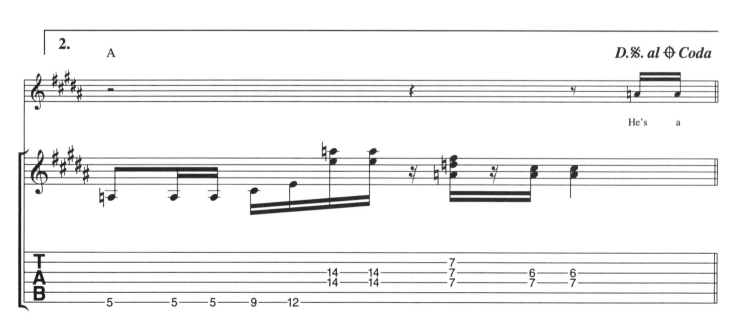

He's   a

Coda ⊕

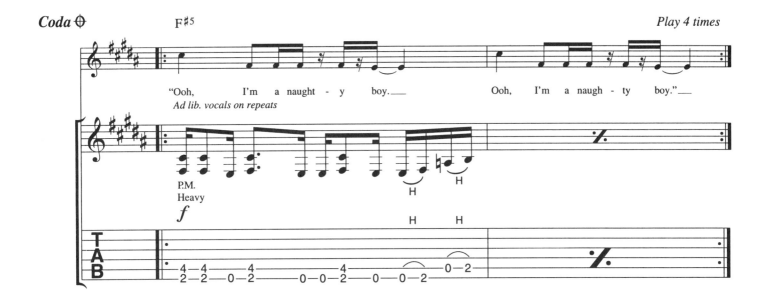

Verse 2:
Mister Robinson and his Quango
Drinks with Generals and County wives
The family business is doing alright
They are doing tangos down in the Quangos
He makes them tick and he makes them tock
And if he don't get it he puts you in the dock.

He just sits in his leather chair and twiddles his thumb
Gets his secretary in and pinches her bum.

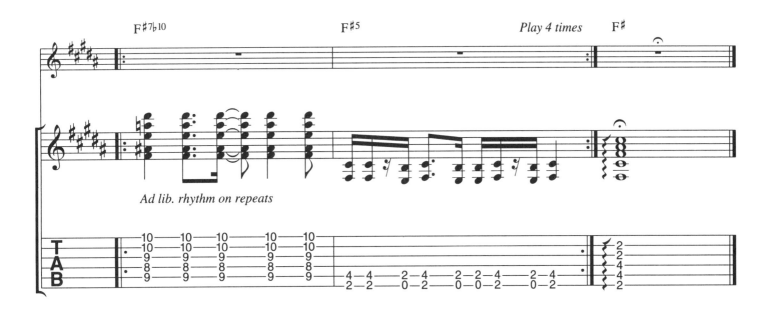

It Could Be You

Words & Music by Damon Albarn, Graham Coxon, Alex James & David Rowntree

73

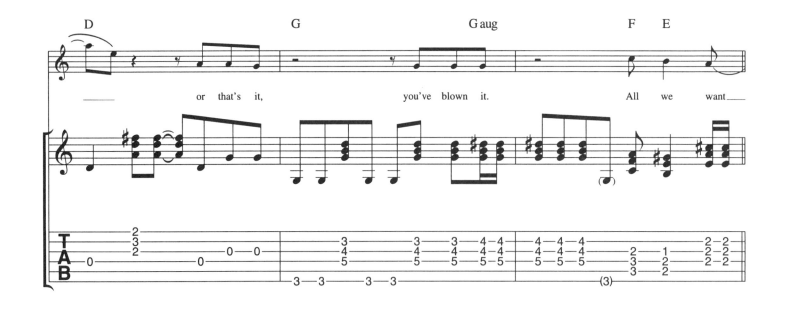

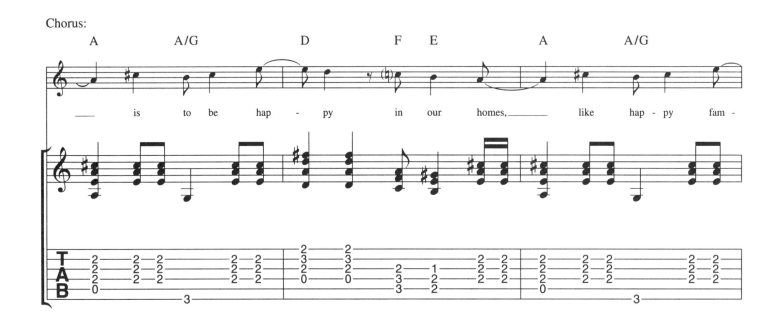

Chorus:

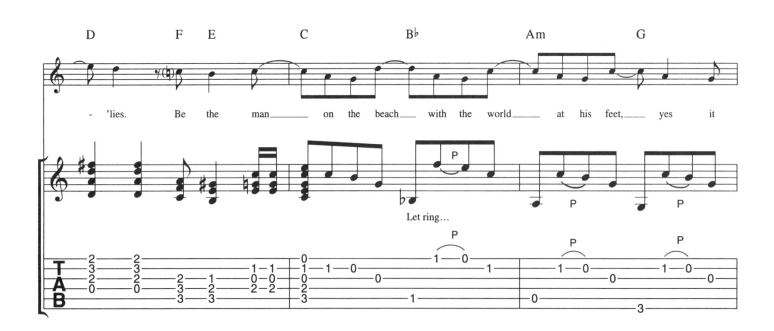

Let ring…

74

Could be me, (could be you,) could be you, (could be you,) could be me, (could be you,) could be you, (could be you.)

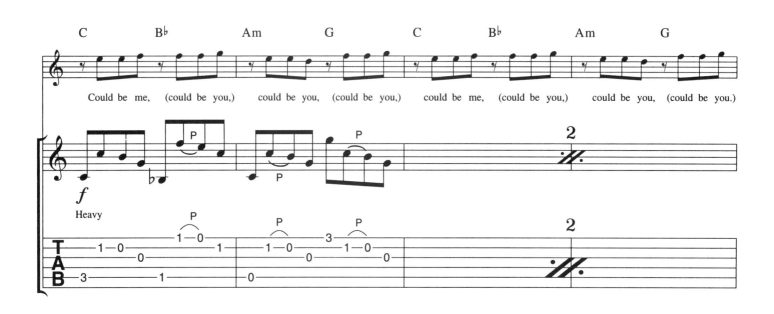

Could be me, (could be you,) could be you, (could be you,) could be me, (could be you,) could be you, (could be you.)

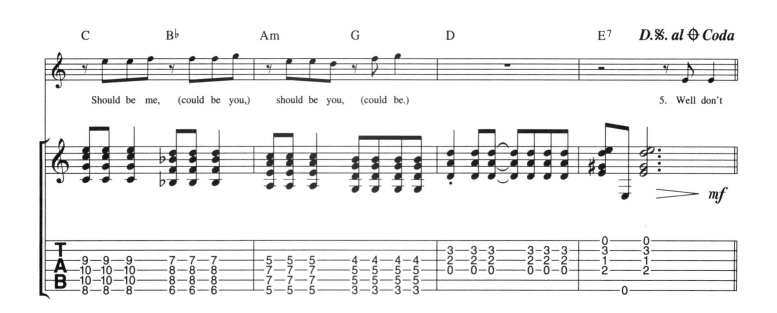

Should be me, (could be you,) should be you, (could be.) 5. Well don't

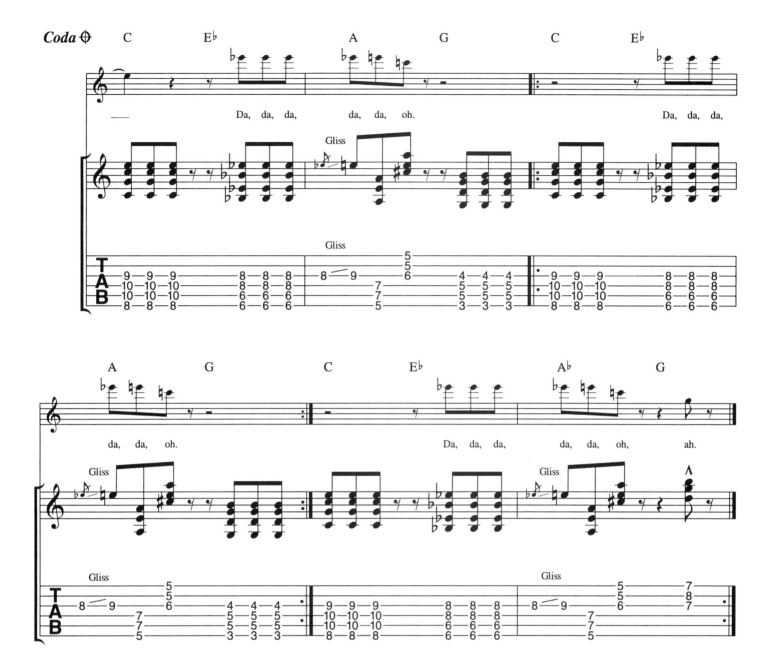

Coda

Verse 3:
The likely lads
Are picking up the uglies
Yesterday they were just puppies
Beery sluts, now life's a blur.

Verse 4:
Telly addicts
You should see them at it
Getting in a panic
Will we be there, Trafalgar Square?

Verse 5(𝄋):
Well don't worry
If it's not your lucky number
Because tomorrow there's another
Could be you, could be me.

He Thought Of Cars

Words & Music by Damon Albarn, Graham Coxon, Alex James & David Rowntree

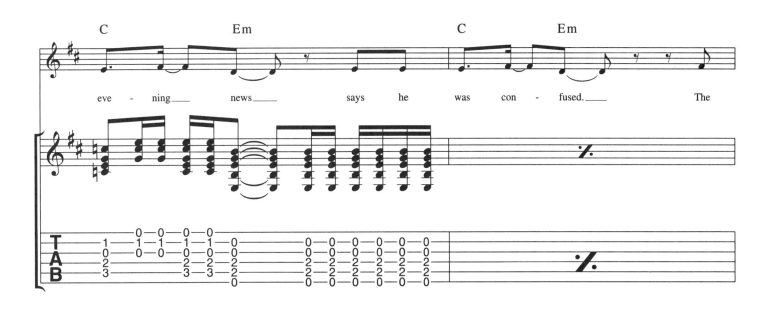

eve - ning___ news___ says he was con - fused.___ The

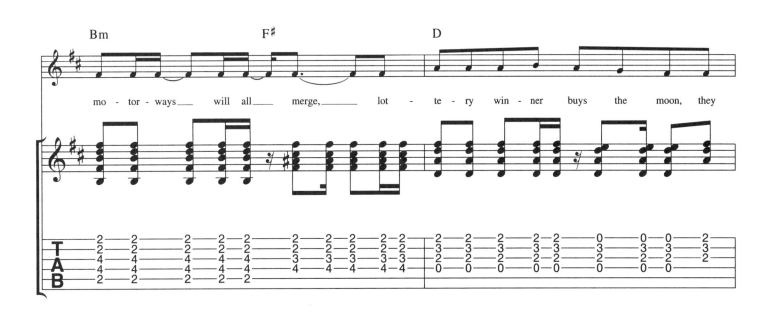

mo - tor - ways___ will all___ merge,___ lot - te - ry win - ner buys the moon, they

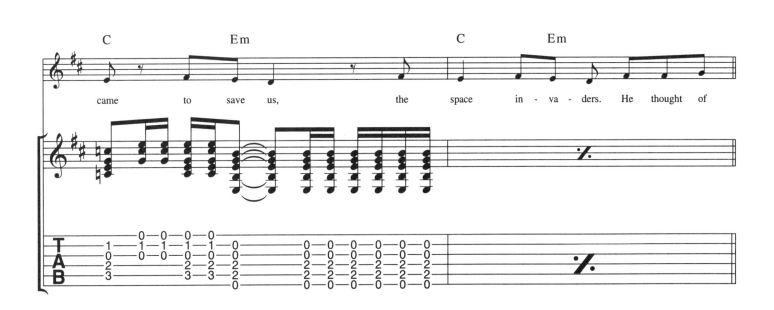

came to save us, the space in - va - ders. He thought of

Chorus:

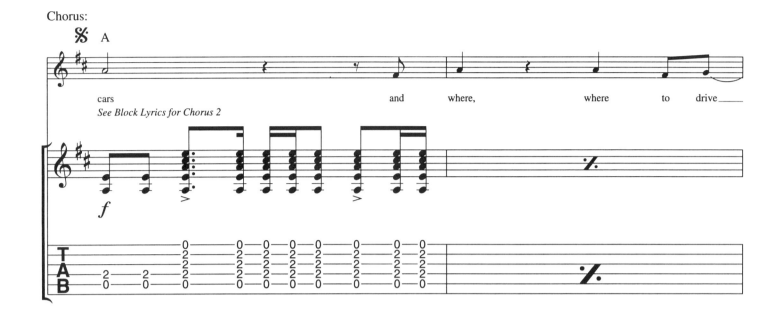

cars
See Block Lyrics for Chorus 2
and where, where to drive_____

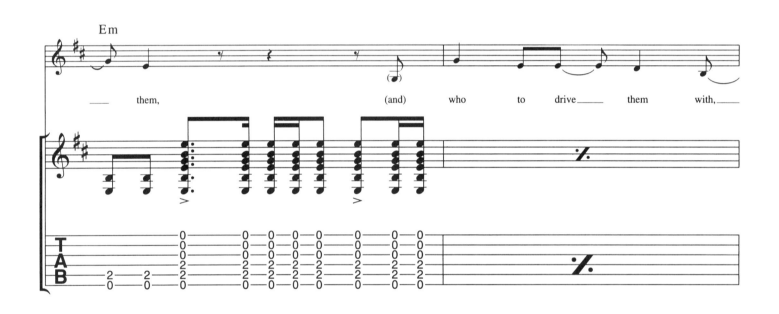

_____ them, (and) who to drive_____ them with,_____

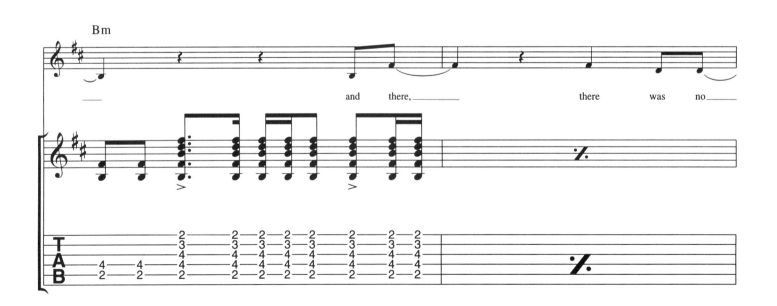

_____ and there,_____ there was no_____

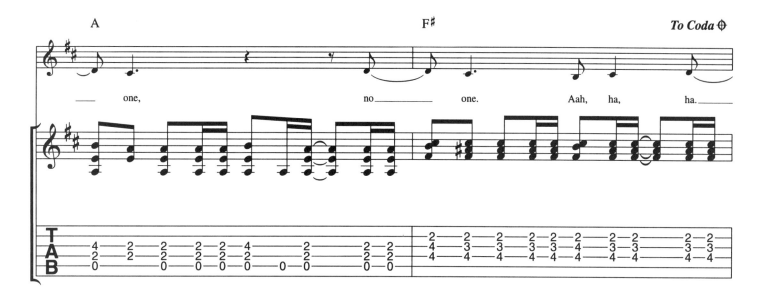

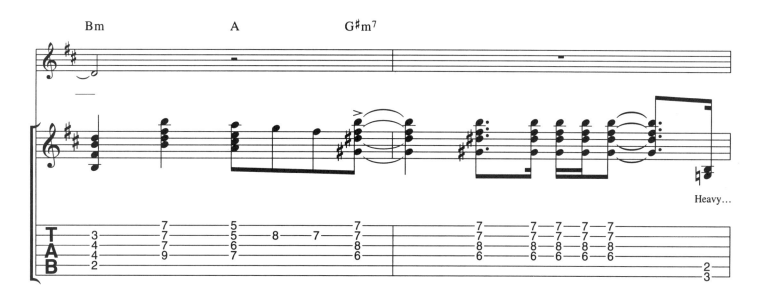

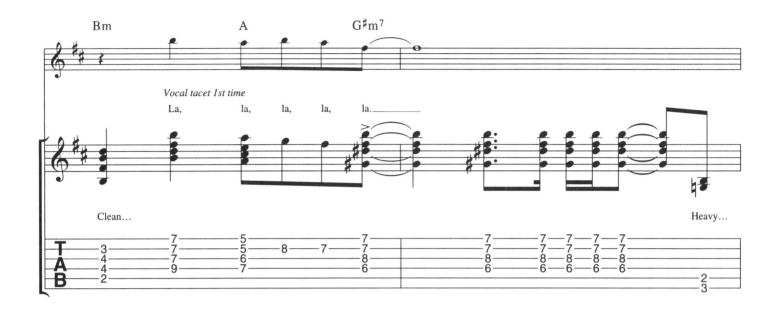

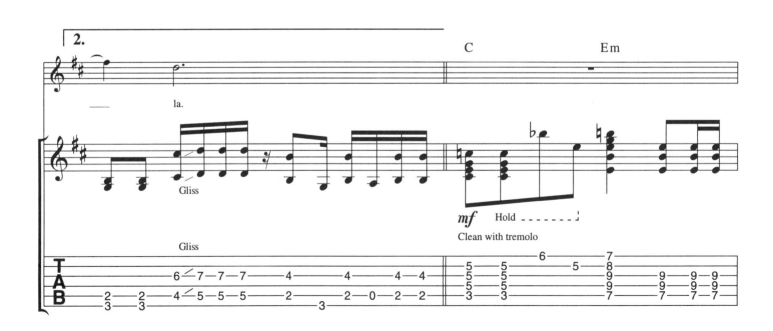

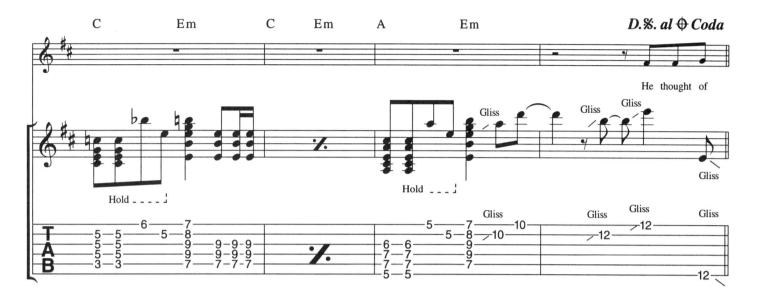

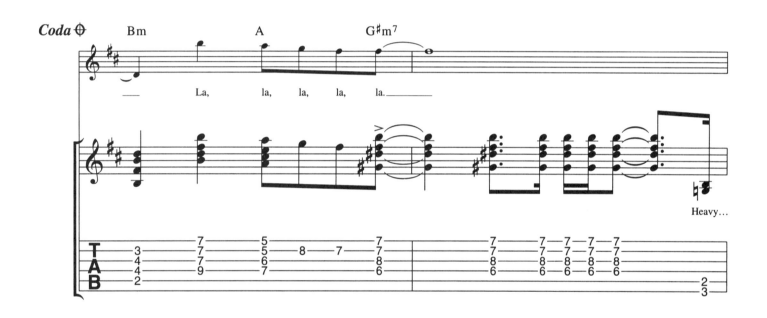

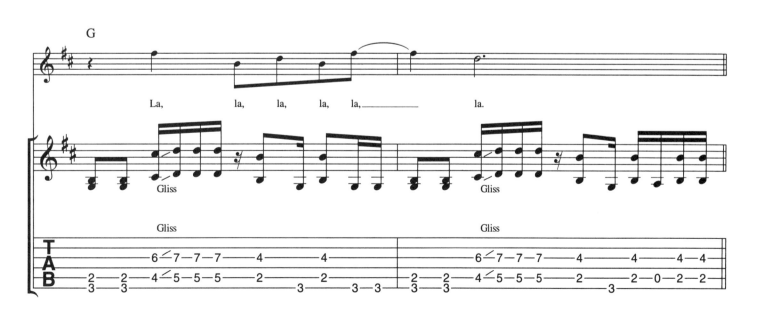

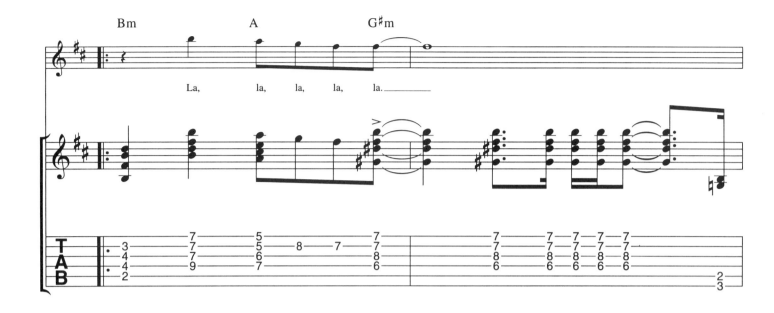

Verse 2:
There's panic at London Heathrow
Everybody wants to go up into the blue
But there's a ten year queue
Colombia is in top gear
It shouldn't snow this time of year
Now America's shot
She's gone and done the lot.

Chorus 2:
He thought of planes
And where, where to fly
And who to fly there with
And there, there was no one, no one.

Ernold Same

Words & Music by Damon Albarn, Graham Coxon, Alex James & David Rowntree

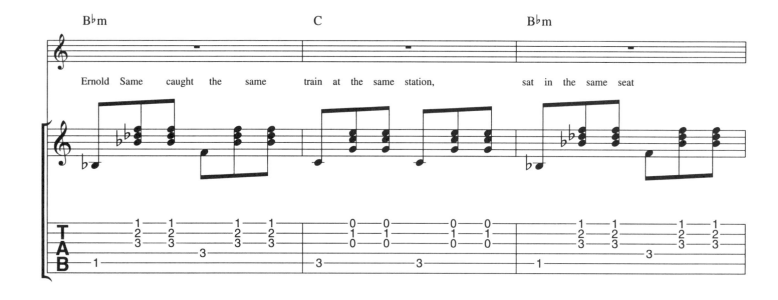

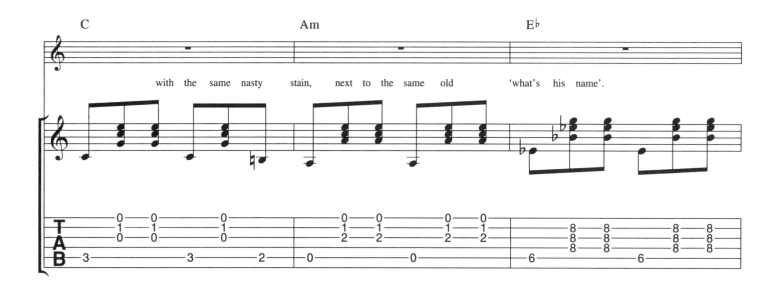

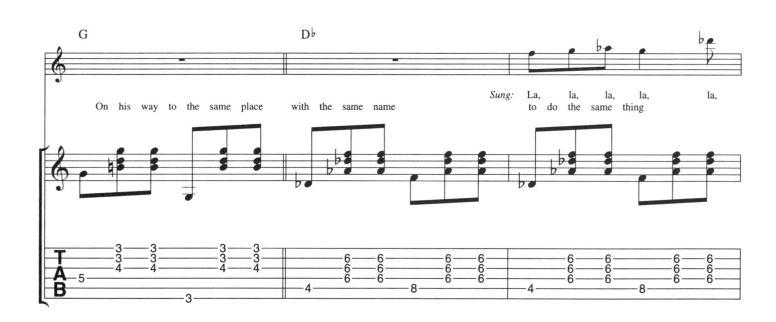

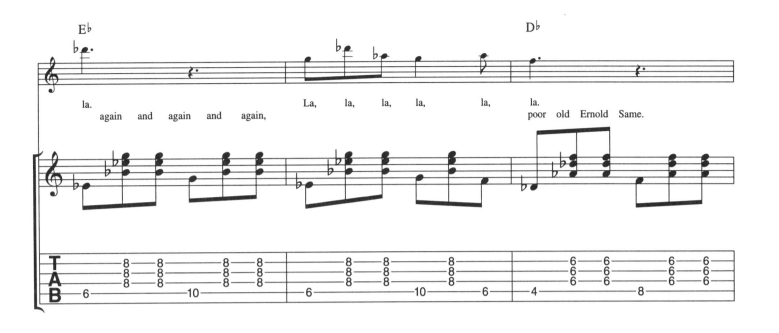

again and again and again, La, la, la, la, la, la. poor old Ernold Same.

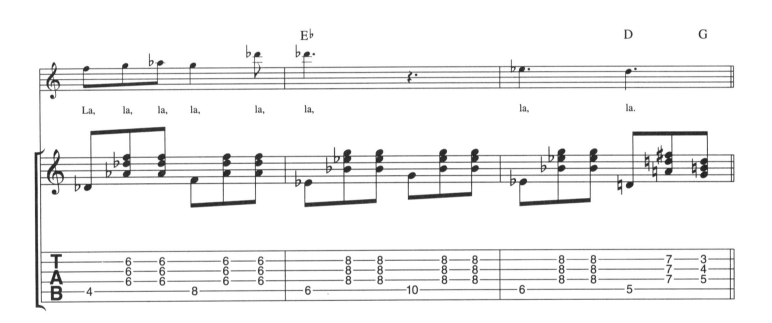

La, la, la, la, la, la, la, la.

Old Ern - old_____ Same,_____ his world stays the_____ same, to -

day ____ will al - ways be to - mor - row.

Poor old Ern - old ____ Same, he's get - ting that feel - ing once a - gain, ____

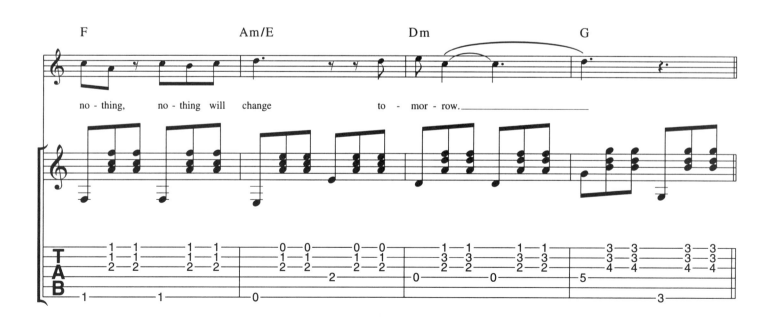

no - thing, no - thing will change to - mor - row. ____

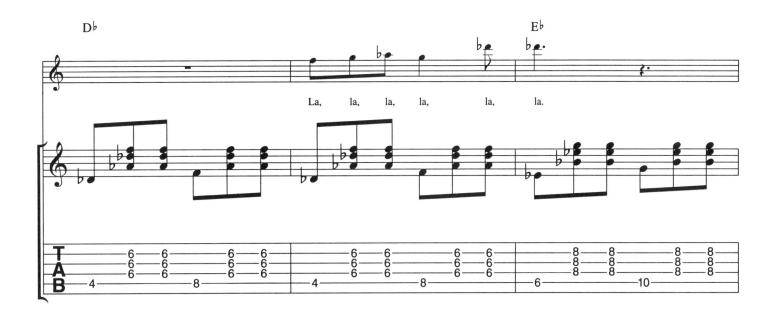

La, la, la, la, la, la.

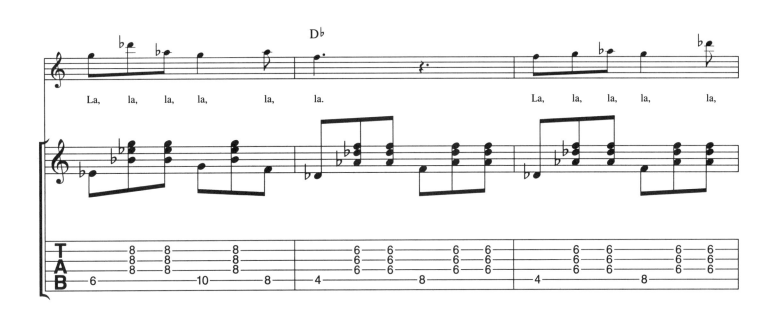

La, la, la, la, la, la. La, la, la, la, la,

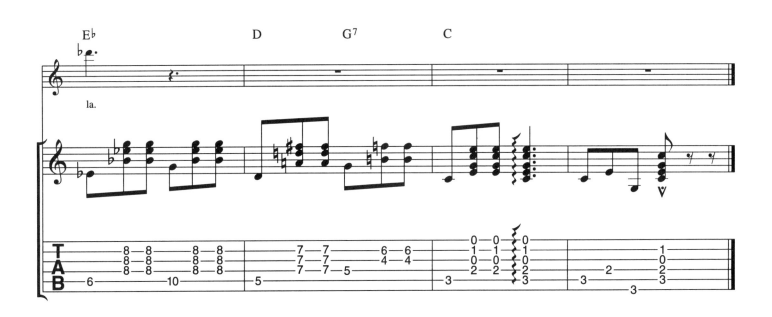

la.

89

Globe Alone

Words & Music by Damon Albarn, Graham Coxon, Alex James & David Rowntree

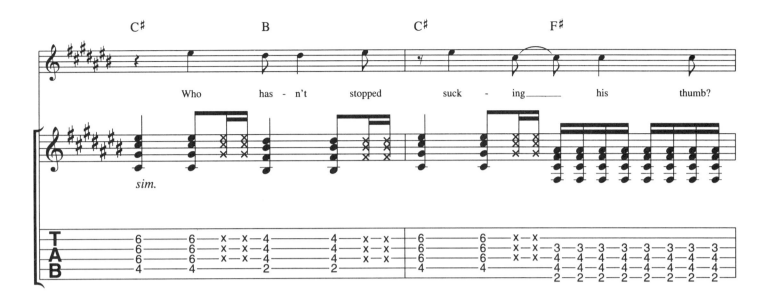

Who has - n't stopped suck - ing_____ his thumb?

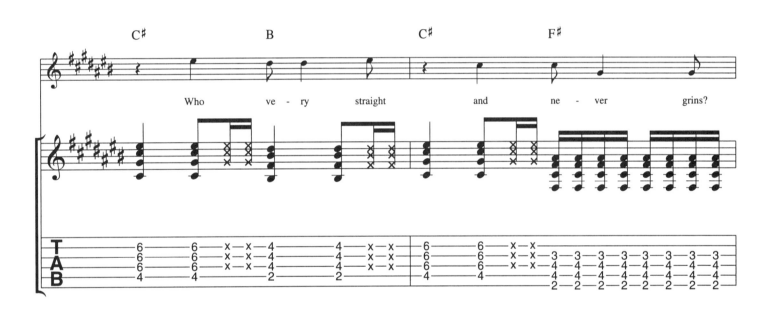

Who ve - ry straight and ne - ver grins?

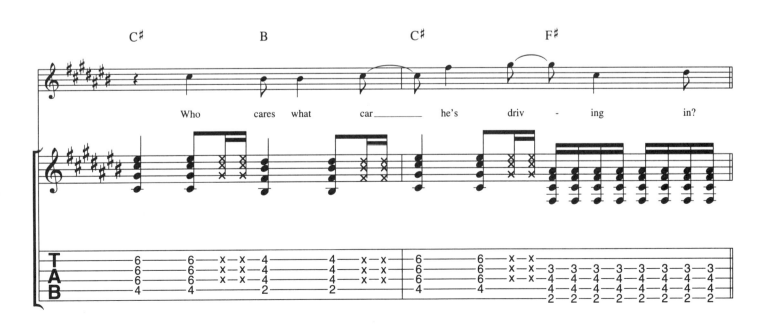

Who cares what car_____ he's driv - ing in?

Chorus:

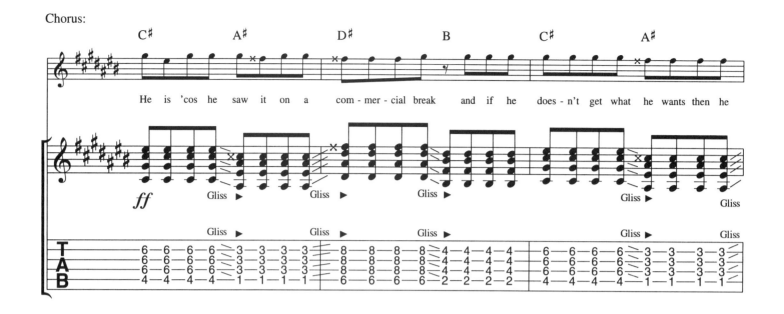

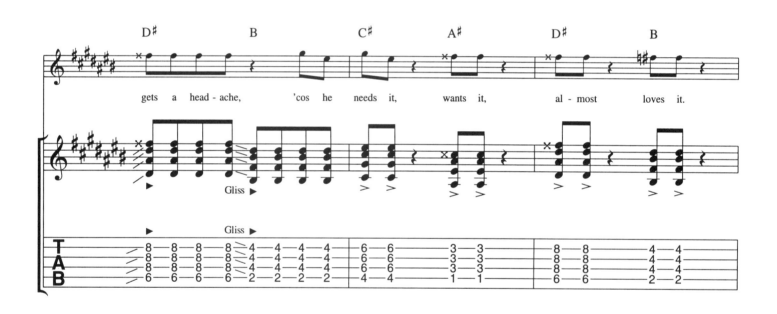

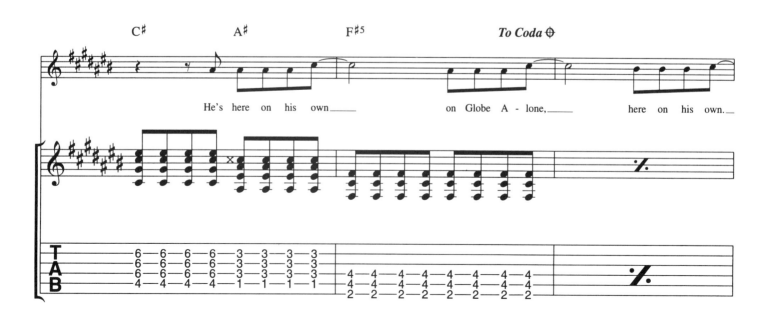

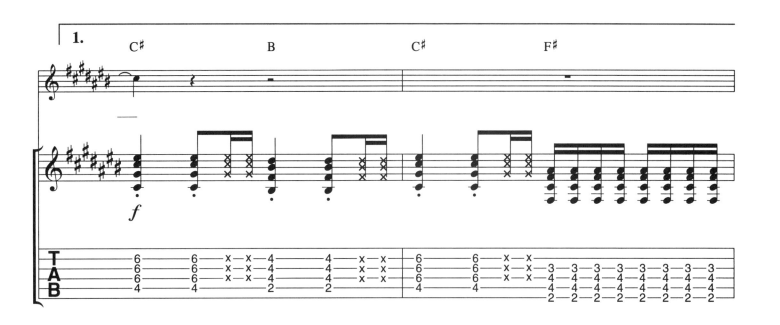

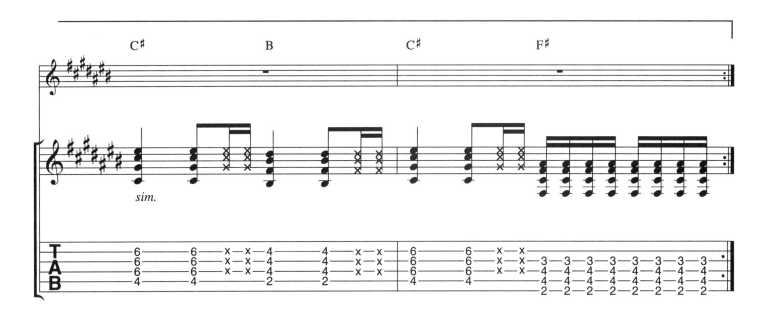

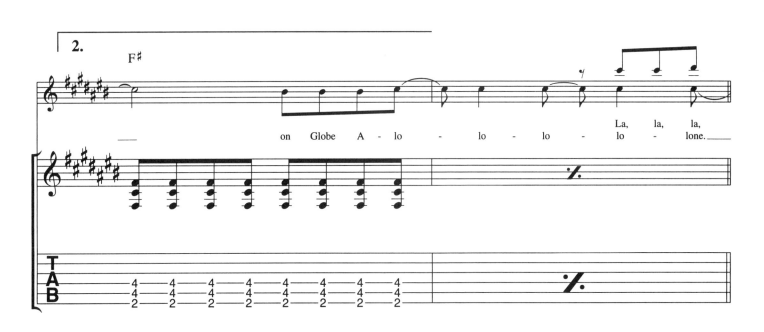

on Globe A - lo - lo - lo - lo - lone. La, la, la,

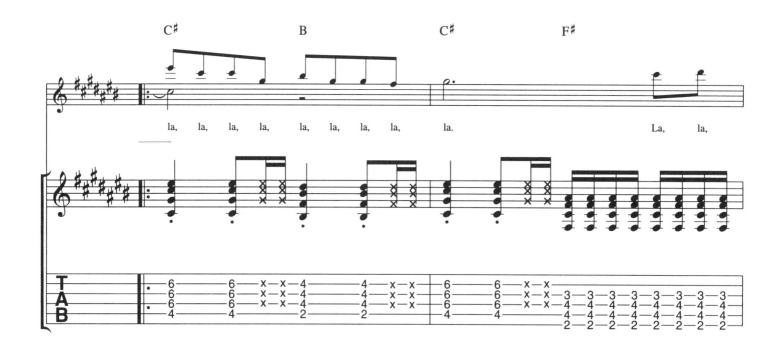

la, la, la, la, la, la, la, la, la. La, la,

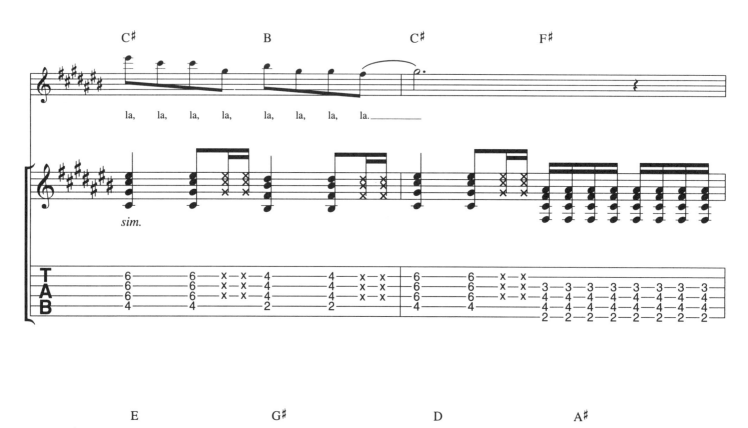

la, la, la, la, la, la, la, la.

sim.

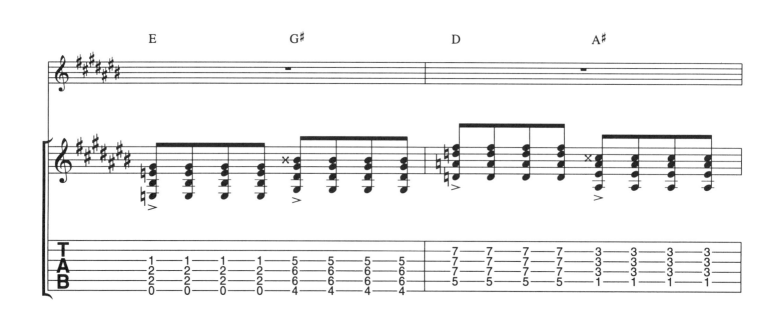

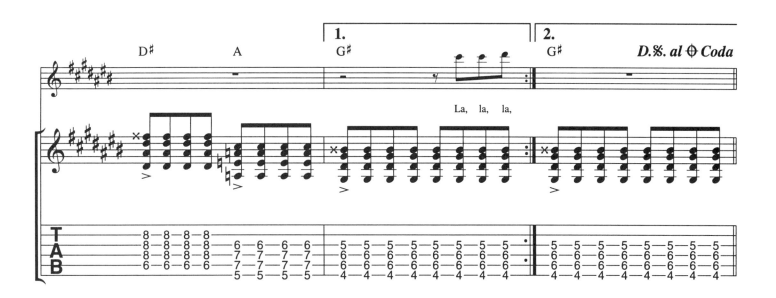

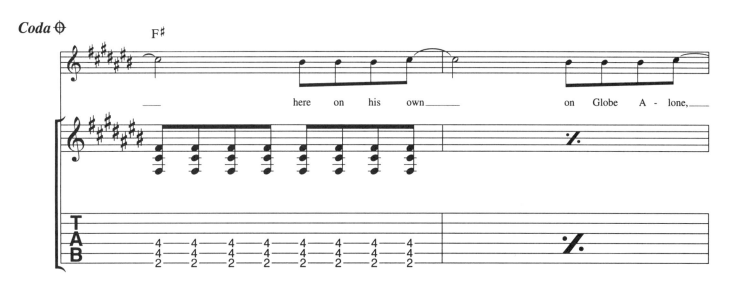

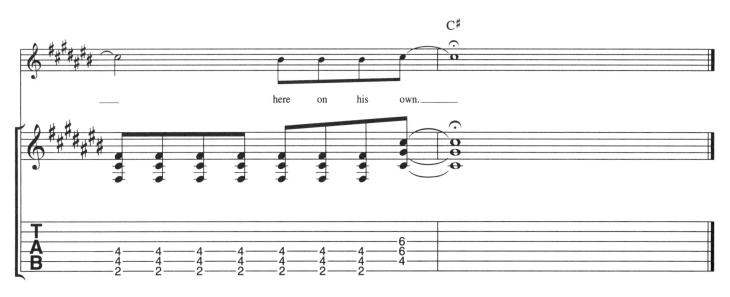

Verse 2:
Who joined health club to glisten?
Into hi-fi precision?
Who mobile phone gives him the bone?
Who very keen on Sharon Stone?

Verse 3(𝄋):
Who only eats at the new brasserie?
Who only ever gets merry?
Who wouldn't be seen at bed time
Without putting Calvin Kleins on?

Dan Abnormal

Words & Music by Damon Albarn, Graham Coxon, Alex James & David Rowntree

Verse:

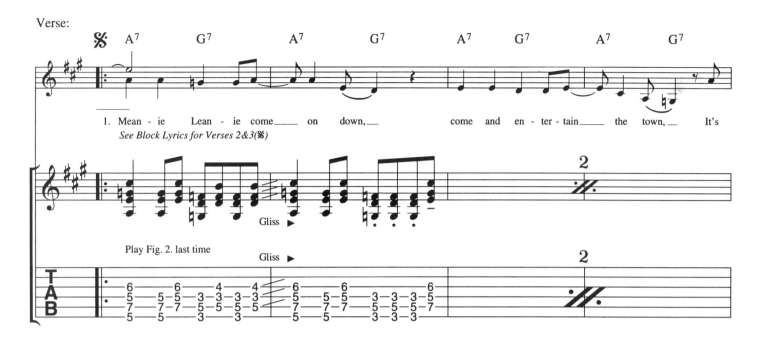

1. Mean - ie Lean - ie come____ on down,___ come and en - ter - tain____ the town, __ It's

See Block Lyrics for Verses 2&3(𝄋)

Play Fig. 2. last time

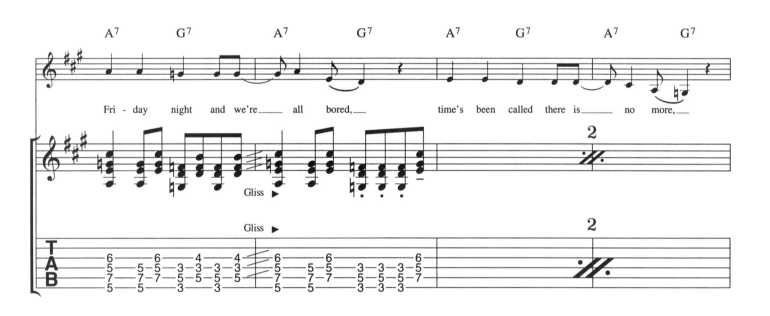

Fri - day night and we're____ all bored,___ time's been called there is____ no more,

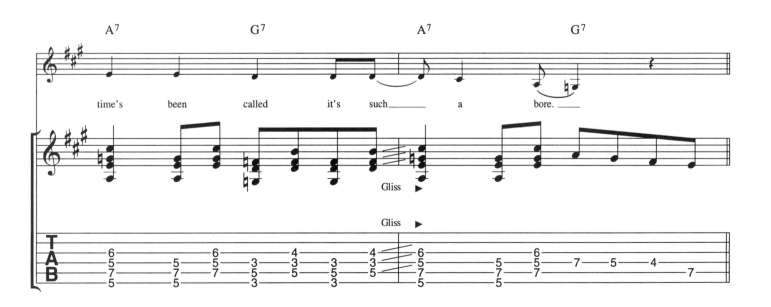

time's been called it's such____ a bore. ___

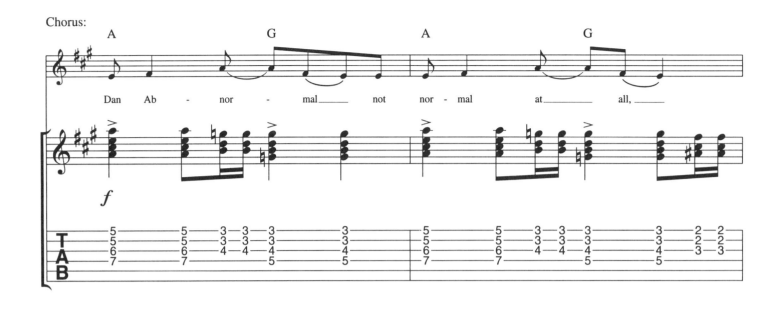

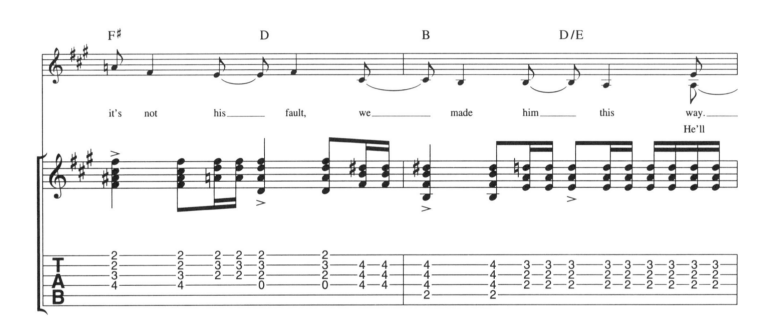

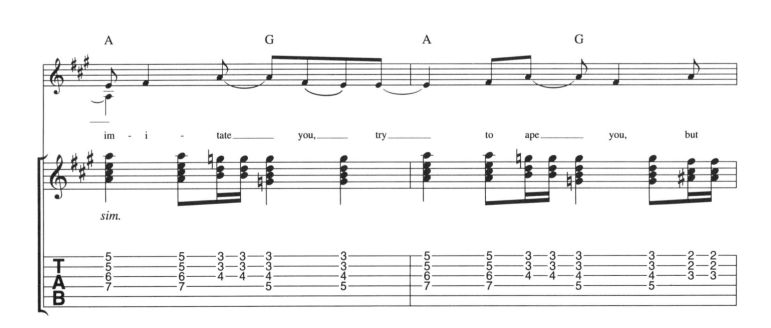

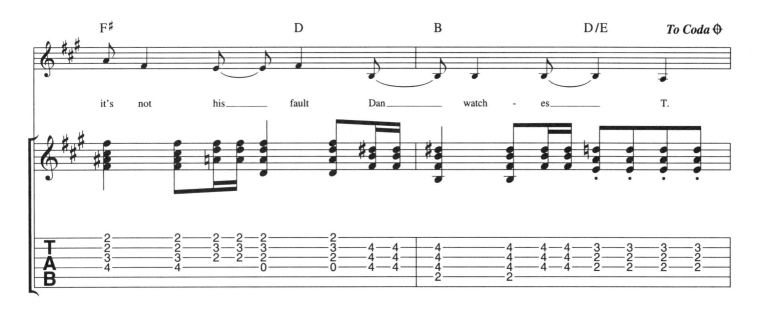

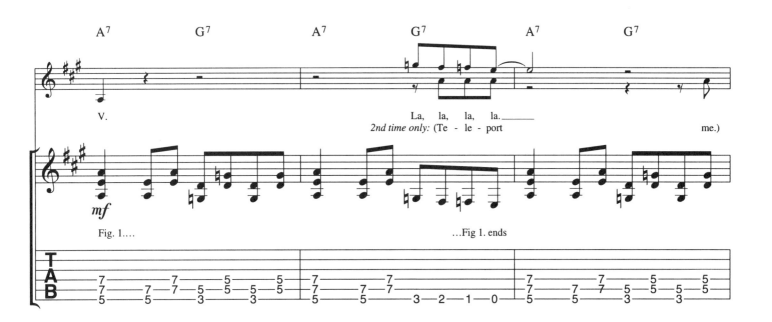

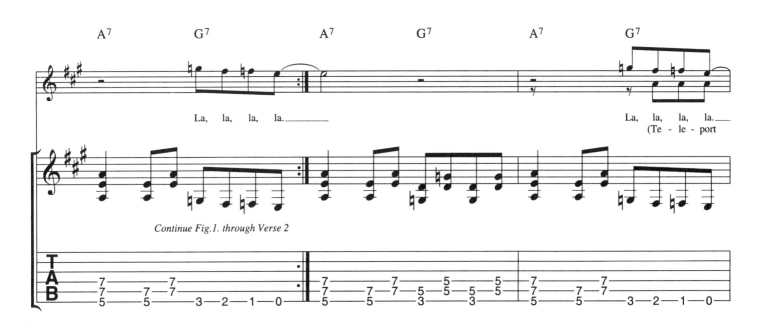

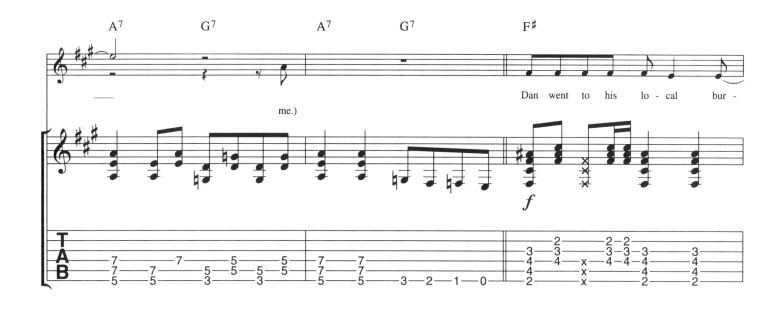

Dan went to his lo - cal bur -

me.)

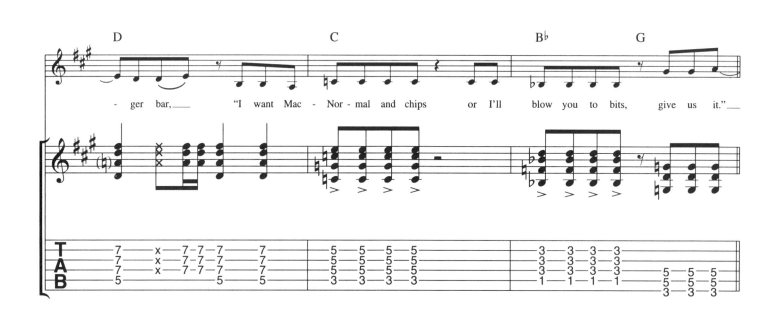

- ger bar, "I want Mac - Nor - mal and chips or I'll blow you to bits, give us it."

Solo:

Fig. 2...   ...Fig. 2. ends

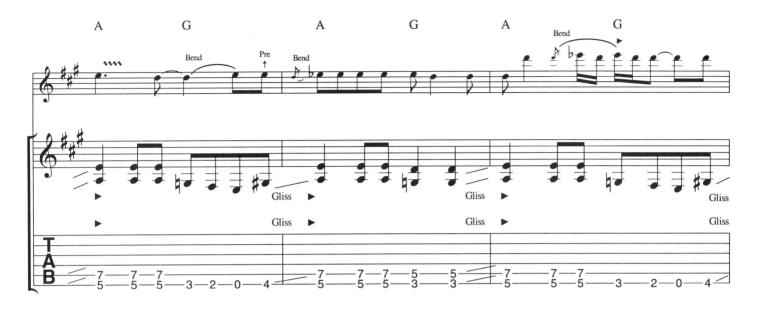

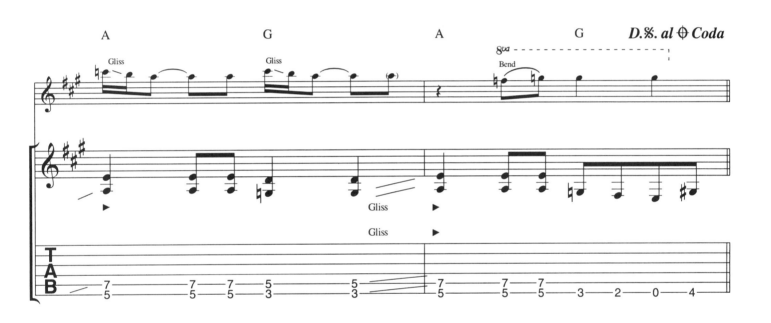

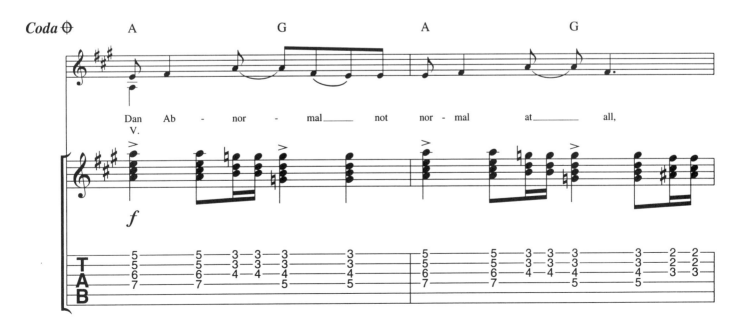

Dan Ab - nor - mal____ not nor - mal at____ all,

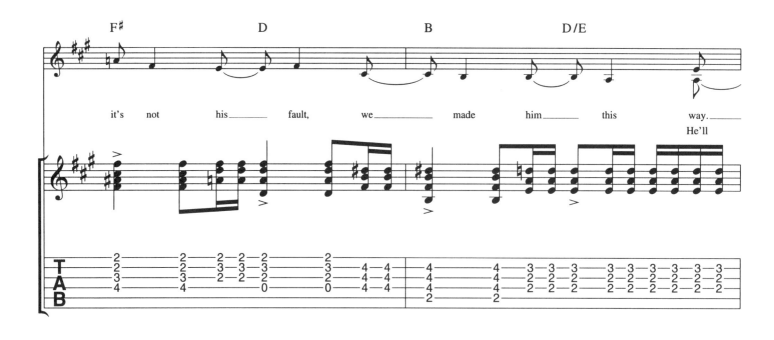

it's not his_____ fault, we_____ made him_____ this way._____
He'll

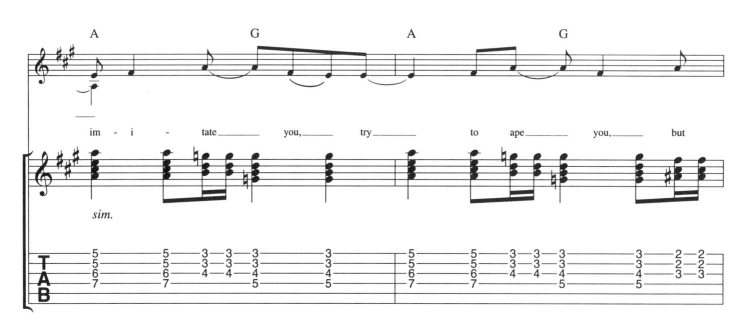

im - i - tate_____ you,_____ try_____ to ape_____ you,_____ but

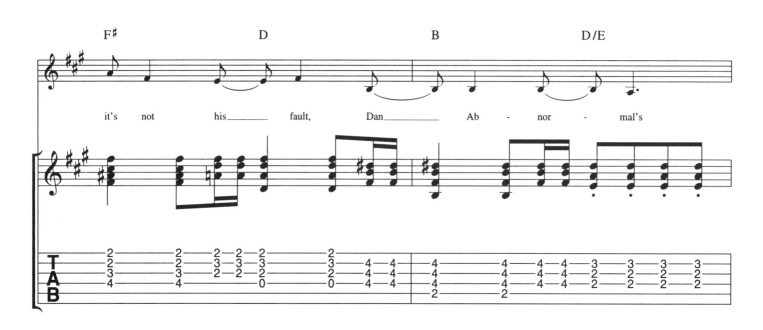

it's not his_____ fault, Dan_____ Ab - nor - mal's

Verse 2:
The Meanie Leanie stays up late
Mopes around, gets in a state
He's the killer in your Arcade
Shooting gangsters ready made
'Cause that is where the future's made.

Verse 3(s):
It's the miseries at half past three
Watching video nasties
Has dirty dreams when he's asleep
'Cos Dan's just like you and me
He's the Meanie Leanie.

Yuko and Hiro

Words & Music by Damon Albarn, Graham Coxon, Alex James & David Rowntree

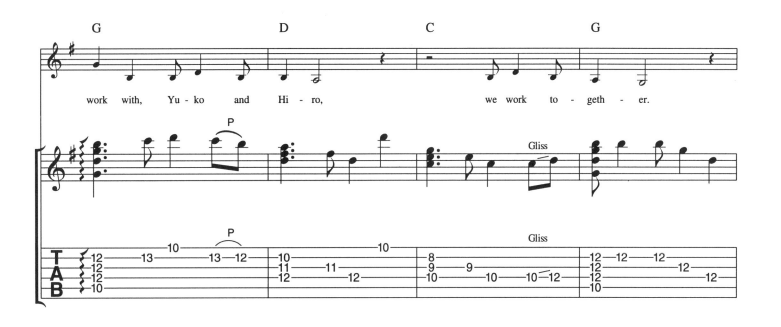

work with, Yu - ko and Hi - ro, we work to - geth - er.

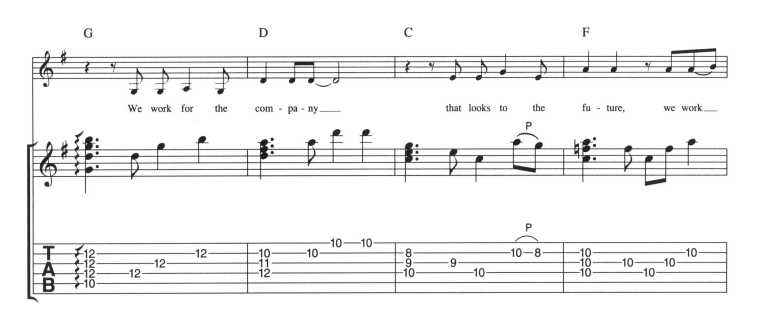

We work for the com - pa - ny___ that looks to the fu - ture, we work___

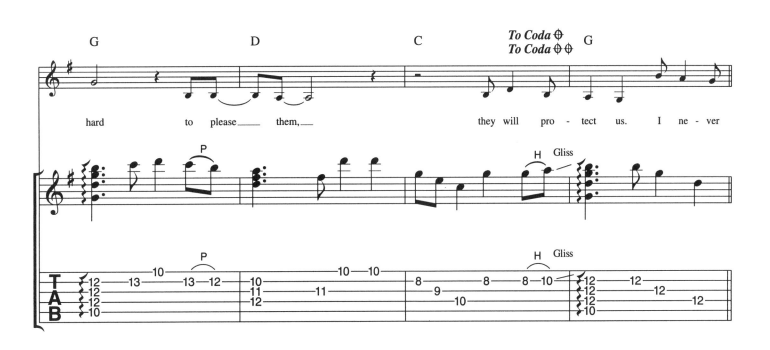

hard to please___ them,___ they will pro - tect us. I ne - ver

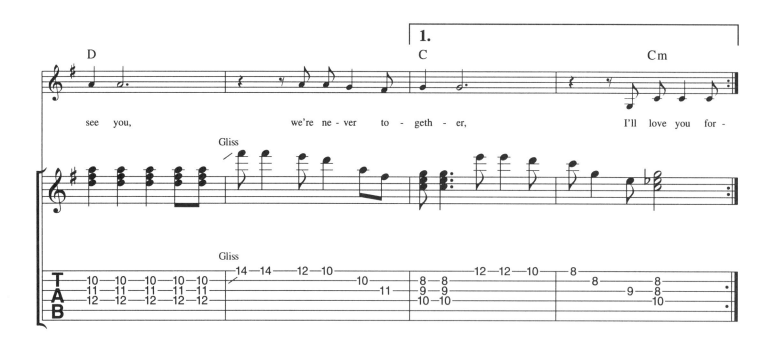

see you,   we're ne - ver   to - geth - er,   I'll love you for -

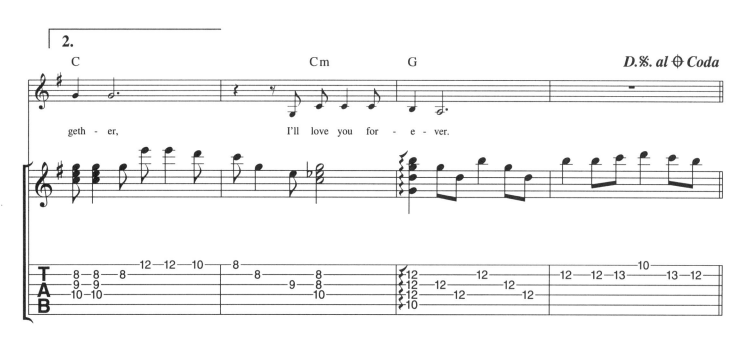

geth - er,   I'll love you for - e - ver.

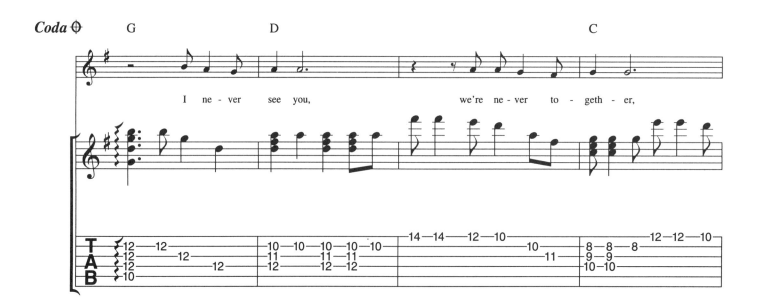

I ne - ver   see you,   we're ne - ver   to - geth - er,

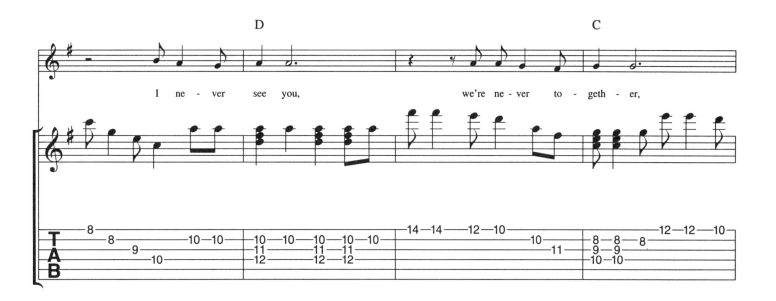

I ne - ver see you, we're ne - ver to - geth - er,

I'll love you for -

+ echoes to fade

Verse 2:
I drink in the evening
It helps with relaxing
I can't sleep without drinking
We drink together.

From Monday to Saturday
I go to my workplace
But on Sunday we're together
Yuko and Hiro
I never see you
We're never together
I'll love you forever.

Verse 3:
Instrumental (ad lib.)

Verse 4(𝄋):
Instrumental

Entertain Me

Words & Music by Damon Albarn, Graham Coxon, Alex James & David Rowntree

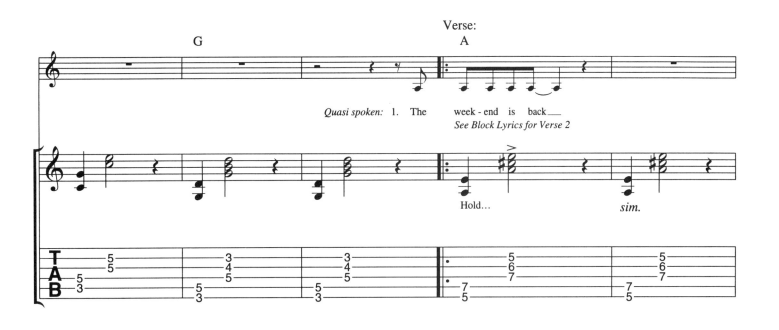

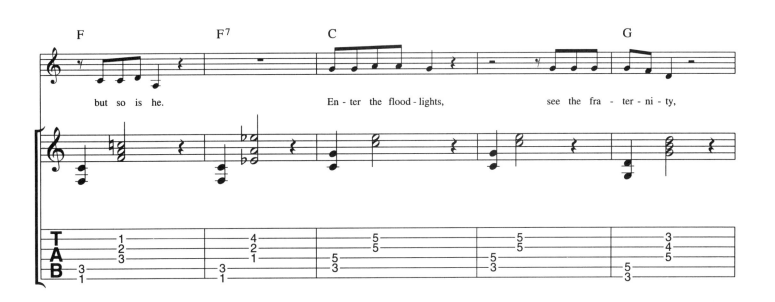

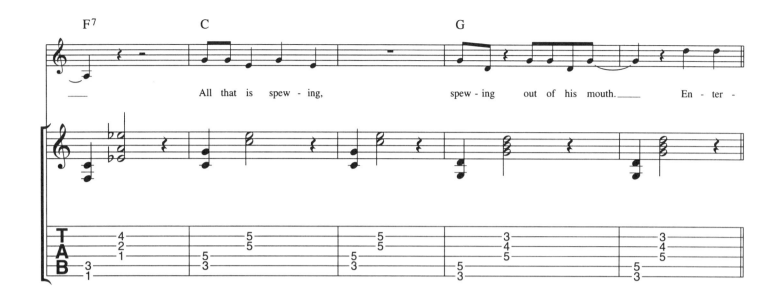

All that is spew - ing, spew - ing out of his mouth._____ En - ter -

Chorus:

tain me,_____ en - ter - tain me,_____ en - ter -

Hold...   sim.

1,3.

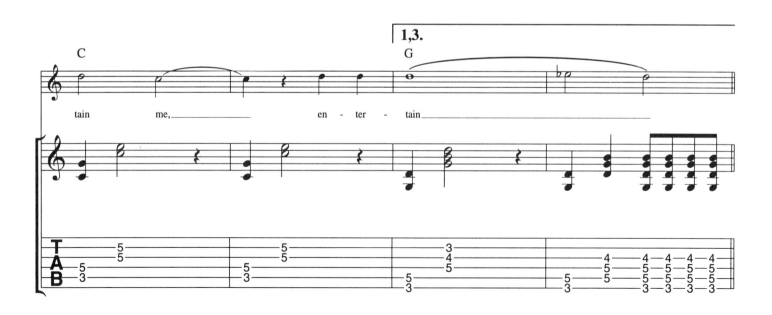

tain me,_____ en - ter - tain_____

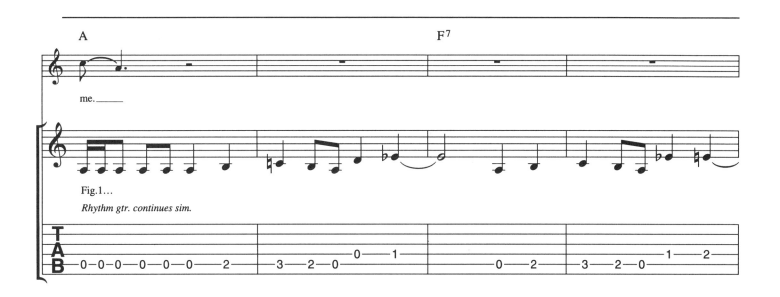

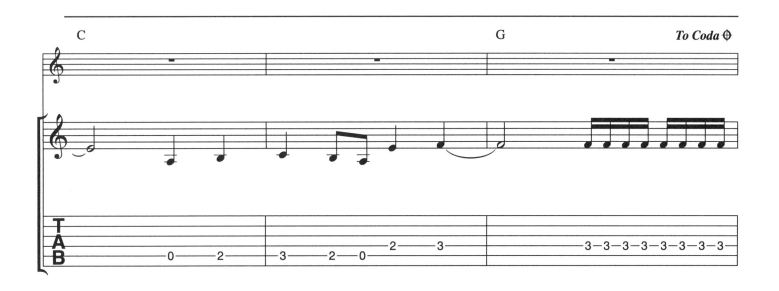

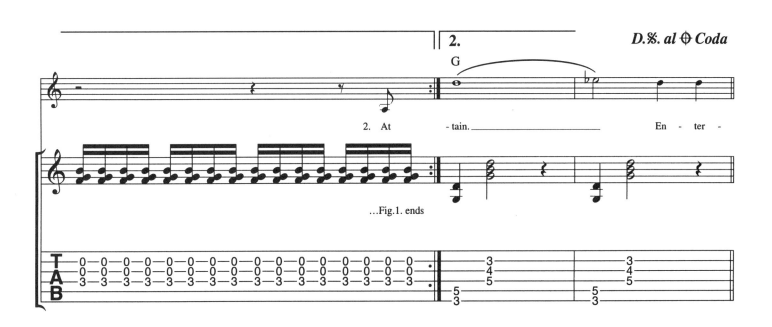

Coda ⊕

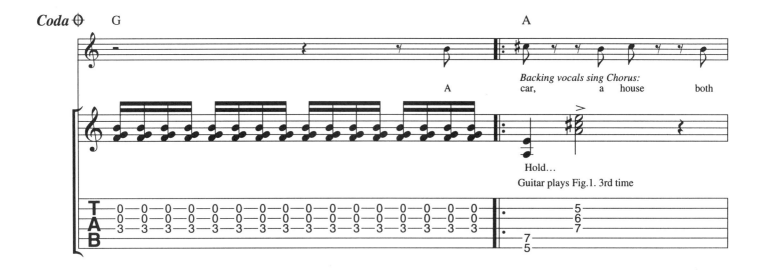

Backing vocals sing Chorus:
car,   a   house   both

Hold…
Guitar plays Fig.1. 3rd time

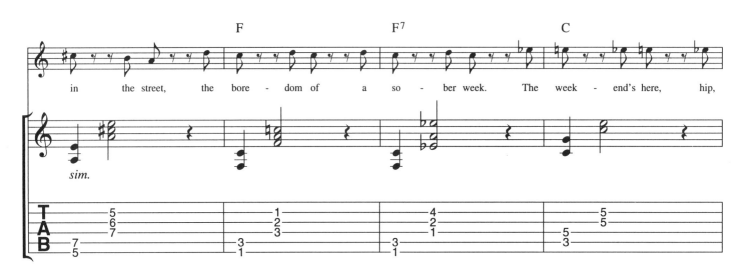

in   the street,   the bore - dom of a so - ber week.   The week - end's here,   hip,

sim.

Repeat ad lib. to fade

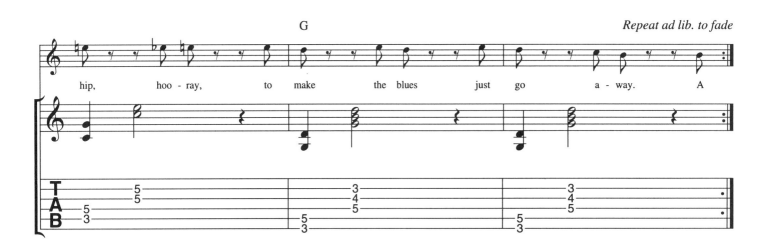

hip,   hoo - ray,   to   make   the blues   just   go   a - way.   A

Verse 2:
At 'His and Her' dating
Bored minds agree
Requirements to be started
Replies awaited
She wants a loose fit
He wants instant whip
He guesstimates her arrival
Will she want it really badly.